SPALDING®

Youth Strength and Conditioning

Matt Brzycki

Coordinator of Health and Fitness,
Strength and Conditioning Programs

Princeton University

MASTERS PRESS

A Division of Howard W. Sams & Co.
A Bell Atlantic Company

Published by Masters Press
(A Division of Howard W. Sams & Co., A Bell Atlantic Company)
2647 Waterfront Pkwy. E. Dr., Suite 300
Indianapolis, IN 46214

Library of Congress Cataloging-in-Publication Data

Brzycki, Matt, 1957 -
    Youth strength and conditioning / Matt Brzycki.
        p. cm. -- (Spalding)
    ISBN 1-57028-041-x (pbk.)
    1. Physical education and training--United States. 2.
Physical fitness--United States. 3. Physical education for
children--United States. 4. Physical fitness for children--United
States.
I. Title. II. Series : Spalding sports library.
GV711.5.B79 1995   95-39332
613.7'11--dc20   CIP

Contents

ACKNOWLEDGMENTS

Special thanks to Daniel Grimaldi, Sasha Ruiz, Courtney Tierney, Brendan Tierney, and Trevor Tierney for volunteering their time as book models.

Additional thanks to Heather Seal, editor of this book, and others from Masters Press for their professional efforts in the production of this book.

Cover design by Christy Pierce.

All photos by Matt Brzycki unless otherwise noted.

This book is dedicated to my wife, Alicia.
I love you very much.

Physical Education courses must offer participation in activities that promote flexibility, aerobic fitness and muscular strength. (photo by Mark Asanovich)

I. THE PAST, PRESENT AND FUTURE

After the end of the second world war, enthusiasm for fitness began to dwindle. The first indication of the decline of the fitness levels of young Americans came in the early stages of the Korean War. The public was alerted to the problem by the publication of the rejection figures of the new draftees. In 1952, the head of the Selective Service reported that 1 1/2 million of the 18 1/2- to 26-year-olds — almost one out of every two young Americans — were rejected for the draft as being mentally, morally or physically unfit.

In December 1953, this anxiety was heightened by the results of a battery of tests — published by Dr. Hans Kraus and Dr. Sonja Weber — which revealed that American youths were not as fit as their European counterparts. The tests were given to 4,458 normal, healthy U.S. school children and 1,987 Austrian and Italian children from comparable urban and suburban communities. These six tests of muscular strength and flexibility were developed from a 15-year study of patients with low back pain at the Posture Clinic of the Columbian Presbyterian Hospital in New York. The tests administered to the youths were identical to those given to the muscularly deficient subjects and, as such, were by no means considered strenuous. Yet, 56.6 percent of the U.S. children failed one or more of the tests while only 8.0 percent of the European children failed.

In response to these much-publicized findings, President Eisenhower formed a President's Council on Youth Fitness in 1956 — the forerunner of the current President's Council on Physical Fitness and Sports. Near the end of 1960, president-elect John F. Kennedy described the results of the so-called "Kraus-Weber Tests" as "the most startling demonstration of the general physical decline of American youth." The Kraus-Weber Tests spawned scores of subsequent fitness tests and research studies that revealed much of the same basic conclusions: American youths were out of shape and overweight.

Many fitness professionals and physical educators feel that today's situation hasn't improved much since the low fitness levels of American youths were first noted in the 1950s. In fact, there are strong indications that the problem has deteriorated even further. For example, a report by the Federal Department of Health and Human Services found that children born in the 1980s are less fit than the children of the 1960s were. In addition, a national survey of 12,000 youths aged 6 to 17 — cosponsored by the Amateur Athletic Union and the Chrysler Fund — found that fewer youths meet minimum standards for aerobic fitness, flexibility and abdominal and upper body strength than in 1981. Two other national surveys reported that at least half of all American school children don't get enough exercise and another study pointed out that up to 20 million youths are overweight. Finally, a 1986 study undertaken by the Public Health Service collected data from 19 states on 4,678 children aged 6 to 9. This study disclosed that youths in this age bracket carried more body fat than did their counterparts of the 1960s.

Clearly, there's no shortage of studies, tests and surveys that indicate American youths have poor levels of fitness. Perhaps the most frightening finding of all was made by the American Alliance for Health, Physical Education, Recreation and Dance. Their 1987 study showed that 40 percent of those youths between the ages of 5 and 8 already have at least one of the four risk factors associated with heart disease: obesity, high blood pressure, elevated cholesterol levels and inactivity.

The Need For Regular Exercise

Just how important is it for youths to participate in regularly scheduled physical activity? Youths who exercise regularly can obtain numerous physical benefits. Regular exercise facilitates the normal growth and development of the muscles, bones and connective tissue. Strengthening these biological components is also an excellent precautionary measure against injury. In addition, young athletes can perform closer to their potential by increasing their functional strength. Conditioning activities can prepare young athletes for the demands of a particular sport. Vigorous physical activity also helps youths to maintain a proper

Youths who exercise regularly can obtain numerous physical benefits. (photo by Raymond Grimaldi)

Physical education courses must offer participation in activities that promote flexibility, aerobic fitness and muscular strength. (photo by Mark Asanovich)

bodyweight and a desirable level of body fat. Furthermore, youths who are physically fit can perform their daily activities without showing signs of undue fatigue. Exercise develops a wide range of motor skills that can be used in everyday functions and leisure pursuits. Most importantly, regular physical activity reduces a youth's risk of experiencing coronary heart disease at a later age.

There are several mental and psychological benefits as well. Regular physical exercise improves self-discipline, self-confidence and self-esteem during the critical identity-forming years. Physically active youths are less prone to emotional disturbances and are generally more outgoing and optimistic. Youths can also use physical activity as an outlet to release tension and stress. Finally, regular exercise increases a youth's alertness and interest in learning.

The "Unfitness Boom"

Unfortunately, the fitness boom of the 1970s and 1980s — which created a widespread appreciation of health and well-being among adults — has not filtered down to youths. Why not? First of all, fitness testing isn't nearly as common nowadays — it was much more routine for children of the '60s . . . and the children of the '60s grew up to be the adults of the fitness boom era. Another reason pertains to the many cultural changes and various technological advancements that have taken place since the 1970s. Today's youths are often charmed and seduced by the ubiquitous television set along with more recent developments such as computers and video games. Quite simply, youths are becoming watchers instead of doers. Additionally, there are a host of products, appliances and transportation that require considerably less energy and effort than in the past and, therefore, have made chores much easier and less time-consuming. Just a few examples are dishwashers, power mowers, electric pencil sharpeners, pocket calculators and motor bikes. Ironically, automation has given youths more leisure time but it has also made them less active. And remember, an inactive youth will probably become an inactive adult.

An additional reason had its genesis during the so-called "Psychedelic '60s" — perhaps the most troubling and turbulent social time America has ever seen. If the United States ever went through a period of adolescence, it was during the decade of the 1960s. Like a young teenager, America struggled to revise its own identity as it grappled with a plethora of domestic conflicts and confrontations concerning such issues as sexual freedom, campus unrest, drug usage, civil rights and political activism. The Vietnam Era also saw a rebellion against authority and conformity that pitted the young against the old thereby creating a generation gap. Students became increasingly disillusioned by a society that they viewed as being overly competitive. Needless to say, physical education came under heavy scrutiny during that time. The basic argument was that students should have more freedom and self-expression in deciding what activities — if any — should be taken.

The aftershocks of this situation can still be felt today. Indeed, maybe the most frequently cited reasons for the low fitness levels of youths have to do with the physical education (PE) in the schools in terms of both quantity and quality. In 1993, there were only four states — Hawaii, Illinois, Kentucky and Rhode Island — that required all students in grades K-12 to take a specific amount of PE courses and only one state — Illinois — required students in grades K-12 to take PE everyday. This isn't very encouraging — especially when you consider that for many students, PE classes represent the day's only physical exercise. Yet, when state and local governments are looking to trim the budgetary fat, usually one of the first programs on the chopping block is physical education.

The quality of the PE programs has also been questioned. It was previously noted that much less fitness testing is conducted today than in the past. The biggest criticism, however, is that schools place entirely too much emphasis on team sports — which has changed physical education to physical competition. The feeling is that PE classes merely cater to the needs of the athletes and do very little for the average students. There's no question that competitive sports can develop many admirable qualities such as teamwork, discipline, self-esteem, camaraderie and sportsmanship. Nevertheless, many feel that PE classes generally do not promote healthy fitness habits or stress lifelong recreational activities such as swimming, cycling, running and tennis.

Correcting The Problem

There are certain steps that can be taken to correct the seemingly abysmal levels of fitness among American youth. To begin with, the quantity and quality of the schools' PE programs must be addressed at the community level. PE courses must be made more frequent and should be required for all students in all grades. The Council on Physical Education for Children of the National Association for Sport and Physical Education —America's largest professional association of children's PE teachers — believes that quality, daily PE should be available to all children. These classes must educate youths so that they gain an understanding and an appreciation of physical fitness. The reasoning is simple: A youth who is taught an understanding and an appreciation for good health will have a better chance of staying healthy. Instruction should include — but not be limited to — such topics as the benefits of regular exercise, the correct way to exercise, nutritional and dietary guidelines and the basics of weight control. The curriculum should also promote more fitness and less competition. Remember, youths need to develop an awareness that fitness is for fun and for a lifetime of health.

PE classes must emphasize lifelong sports/activities along with the recreational aspects of exercise. The courses must also offer more participation in those activities that promote flexibility, aerobic fitness and muscular strength.

Flexibility

Youths should perform stretching exercises daily to maintain or improve flexibility. These exercises must address the major muscle groups. Each stretch should be held statically for about 30-60 seconds without any bouncing, bobbing or jerking movements. (Guidelines for a safe and comprehensive flexibility program are given in Chapter 2.)

Aerobic Fitness

Aerobic fitness is best developed by activities that are continuous in nature and involve relatively large amounts of muscle mass. Running, swimming, cycling, skating, hiking and rowing are a few excellent examples. These aerobic activities should be performed at a frequency, intensity and duration that is appropriate for the youth's level of physical maturation. (Chapter 3 presents detailed information on developing aerobic fitness.)

Muscular Strength

Although weight training exercises are best for increasing muscular strength, such activities are usually inappropriate for those younger than about 13 or 14. In the case of younger and physically immature teens along with youths having a relatively low level of fitness, calisthenic-type movements can be performed that involve their bodyweight as resistance (such as push-ups and sit-ups). These movements are quite effective for building strength without placing an inordinate amount of stress on their bones and joints. When weight training is done by youths, the exercises should be performed throughout a full range of motion with a controlled speed of movement. The repetitions should be relatively high to reduce the orthopedic stress. The exercises should involve the major muscle groups (i.e., the hips, the legs and the upper torso) and be performed at a frequency, intensity and duration that is appropriate for the youth's level of physical maturation. (Chapters 4 and 5 offer information on developing, designing and revising a safe, efficient strength training program; Chapters 7-14 describe the proper performance of 37 strength training exercises.)

Fitness Testing

Several organizations — including the American College of Sports Medicine (ACSM) and the American Academy of Family Physicians — recommend that students undergo periodic fitness testing. In particular, the ACSM recommends tests of aerobic fitness (running an age-appropriate distance), body composition (measuring skinfolds), muscular strength/endurance (completing pull-ups, push-ups and bent-knee sit-ups or modified versions of those exercises) and flexibility (performing a sit-and-reach or a V-sit). Without a doubt, such testing in PE classes is necessary to ascertain the fitness levels of youths, to monitor improvements and to encourage future involvement. Furthermore, these tests can identify those youths with substandard levels of fitness so that they may receive extra attention.

The Parental Role

Lastly, parents must understand that changing the direction of youth fitness is not just the sole responsibility of the school. The National Children and Youth Fitness Study II suggests that, on the average, parents exercise with their children less than one day a week. The study also revealed that youths who had physically active parents — especially parents who exercised with them — tended to be leaner than youths whose parents were less active. The message is clear: Parents are encouraged to take an active role in participating with their children.

The Future

Remember, a positive change in youth fitness won't happen overnight nor will it happen by itself. But if families, schools and communities band together to provide comprehensive fitness programming today, a powerful stride can be taken toward ensuring that youths become more fit and gain lifelong habits for tomorrow.

II. STRETCHING THE MUSCLES

Flexibility can be defined as the range of motion throughout which a joint can move. The best way to maintain — or improve — a joint's range of motion is to perform specific flexibility movements to stretch the surrounding muscles. Flexibility movements are undoubtedly the simplest and most effortless physical activity to perform — the exertion level is quite low and relaxation is an absolute requirement. Nevertheless, stretching the muscles is one of the most difficult things to get youths to do on their own.

Increasing flexibility serves several purposes. First of all, a more flexible youth will generally be less susceptible to injury. Secondly, a youth will be able to exert strength over a greater range of motion. Finally, stretching the muscles is a way of relieving and/or preventing general muscle soreness.

Flexibility Parameters

There is a distinct relationship between age and the degree of flexibility. The greatest increase in flexibility usually occurs up to and between the ages of 7 and 12. During early adolescence, flexibility tends to level off and thereafter begins to decline. Females are generally more flexible than males.

Although youths are usually quite flexible, it's important to understand that flexibility is affected by several inherited characteristics, particularly the ratio of muscle-to-fat and the insertion points of the muscles. A youth's flexibility also has structural limitations including bones, tendons, ligaments and skin. Finally, it should be noted that flexibility is joint-specific — a high degree of flexibility in one joint doesn't necessarily indicate high flexibility in other joints.

Warming Up

For years, "warming up" was synonymous with stretching. However, warming up and stretching are two separate entities and must be treated as such. A warm-up should precede the flexibility training. Warm-up activities usually consist of low intensity movements such as light jogging or calisthenics. Regardless of the warm-up activity, the idea is to systematically increase the blood circulation and the body temperature. Breaking a light sweat during the warm-up indicates that the body temperature has been raised sufficiently and that the youths are ready to begin stretching their muscles.

By the way, there's no need to stretch or warm-up prior to strength training — provided that a relatively high number of repetitions are performed and the weight is lifted in a controlled manner. However, warming up prior to an activity involving rapid muscle contractions — such as sprinting — is advisable to reduce the risk of injury.

Seven Stretching Strategies

Like all other forms of exercise, stretching movements have certain guidelines that must be followed in order to make the stretches safe and effective. Applying these guidelines will permit youths to maintain or increase their current range of motion. Additionally, they'll be less likely to get injured and will perform closer to their performance potential.

1. Stretch under control without bouncing, bobbing or jerking movements. Bouncing during the stretch actually makes it more painful and increases the risk of tissue damage.
2. Inhale and exhale normally during the stretch without holding the breath. Holding the breath elevates the blood pressure which disrupts the balance and breathing mechanisms.
3. Each stretch should be easy and pain-free. Pain is an indication that the stretching is at or near a youth's structural limits.

4. Relax during the stretch. Relaxing mentally and physically will allow a youth to stretch the muscles throughout a greater range of motion.
5. Hold each stretch for 30-60 seconds. As the flexibility program progresses, the duration of each stretch should be increased.
6. Attempt to stretch a little bit farther than the last time. Progressively increasing the range of motion will improve flexibility.
7. Flexibility work should be done on a regular basis. Youths should stretch at least once a day, especially before a practice, game, conditioning session, PE class or any other activity that will involve explosive, ballistic movements.

Flexibility Exercises

The following pages describe 14 flexibility movements. Each movement lists the muscle(s) stretched, a brief description for each movement and performance points on making the stretch safer and more effective. (For help in identifying the muscles, an anatomy chart is shown in the appendix.) The stretches described in this chapter are the neck forward, neck backward, lateral neck, scratch back, handcuff, standing calf, tibia stretch, sit-and-reach, V-sit, lateral reach, butterfly, spinal twist, quad stretch and knee pull. There are many variations of these stretches that involve the same muscle groups. As such, the stretching program may be individualized to meet personal preferences.

NECK FORWARD

Muscles stretched: neck extensors, trapezius

Description: Interlock the fingers behind the head and slowly pull the chin to the chest.

Performance Points:
- Youths must be especially careful when performing this stretch since the cervical area is involved.
- This movement may also be performed sitting.

NECK BACKWARD

Muscles stretched: sternocleidomastoideus

Description: Place the hands underneath the chin and slowly push the head backward.

Performance Points:
- Youths must be especially careful when performing this stretch since the cervical area is involved.
- This movement may also be performed sitting.

LATERAL NECK

Muscles stretched: sternocleidomastoideus (one side)

Description: Place the right hand on the left side of the head and slowly pull the head to the right shoulder. Repeat the stretch for the right side of the neck.

Performance Points:
- Youths must be especially careful when performing this stretch since the cervical area is involved.
- This movement may also be performed sitting.

SCRATCH BACK

Muscles stretched: upper back (lats), triceps, obliques

Description: Place the left hand on the upper part of the back (behind the head), grab the left elbow with the right hand and slowly pull the upper torso to the right. Repeat the stretch for the right side of the body.

Performance Points:
- For this stretch to be most effective, the hips should not move and the feet should remain flat on the ground.
- Youths should try to gradually reach farther down the back during the stretch.
- This movement may also be performed sitting.
- This movement may be contraindicated for youths with shoulder impingement syndrome.

HANDCUFF

Muscles stretched: chest, anterior deltoid, biceps

Description: Place the hands behind the back, interlock the fingers and slowly lift the hands up as high as possible.

Performance Points:
- A partner may assist in providing a greater stretch by carefully lifting up the hands of the youth doing the stretch.
- This movement may also be performed sitting.

STANDING CALF

Muscles stretched: calves, iliopsoas

Description: While standing upright, step forward with the right foot. Bend the right leg at the knee but keep the left leg straight and the left foot flat on the ground. Repeat the stretch for the right leg.

Performance Points:

- For this stretch to be most effective, the heel of the back foot should remain flat on the ground and both feet should be pointed forward.

TIBIA STRETCH

Muscles stretched: dorsi flexors

Description: Kneel down on the left knee so that the upper leg is perpendicular to the ground while the lower leg and the top part of the foot is flat on the ground. Position the right leg so that the upper leg is parallel to the ground, the lower leg is perpendicular to the ground and the foot is flat on the ground. Repeat the stretch for the right dorsi flexors.

Performance Points:

• For this stretch to be most effective, the top part of the foot being stretched should be flat on the ground.

SIT-AND-REACH

Muscles stretched: buttocks, hamstrings, calves, upper back (lats), lower back

Description: Straighten the legs, put them together and point the toes upward. Slowly reach forward as far as possible without bending the legs.

Performance Points:
- For this stretch to be most effective, the legs should re-main straight and the toes should be pointed upward.
- Youths can progressively stretch farther by reaching for the ankles, the toes and finally the instep.
- A partner may assist in providing a greater stretch by care-fully pushing on the upper back of the youth doing the stretch.
- This movement may also be performed standing (with the legs straight and the arms hanging straight down).

V-SIT

Muscles stretched: buttocks, hip adductors (inner thigh), hamstrings, calves, upper back (lats), lower back

Description: Straighten the legs, spread them apart as far as possible and point the toes upward. Slowly reach forward as far as possible without bending the legs.

Performance Points:

- For this stretch to be most effective, the legs should remain straight and the toes should be pointed upward.
- Youths can progressively stretch farther by "walking" the fingers forward.
- A partner may assist in providing a greater stretch by carefully pushing on the upper back of the youth doing the stretch.
- This movement may also be performed standing (with the legs spread apart and the arms hanging straight down).

LATERAL REACH

Muscles stretched: buttocks, hip adductors (inner thigh), hamstrings, calves, upper back (lats), obliques, lower back

Description: Straighten the legs, spread them apart as far as possible and point the toes upward. Slowly reach down the left leg as far as possible without bending the legs. Repeat the stretch for the other side of the body.

Performance Points:
- For this stretch to be most effective, the legs should remain straight and the toes should be pointed upward.
- Youths can progressively stretch farther by "walking" the fingers forward.
- A partner may assist in providing a greater stretch by carefully pushing on the upper back of the youth doing the stretch.
- This movement may also be performed standing (with the legs spread apart and the arms reaching down the leg).

BUTTERFLY

Muscles stretched: hip adductors (inner thigh), lower back

Description: Place the soles of the feet together, draw the heels as close to the buttocks as possible and place the elbows on the insides of the knees. Bend the torso forward while slowly pushing down with the elbows against the knees.

Performance Points:
• A partner may assist in providing a greater stretch by carefully pushing on the insides of the knees of the youth doing the stretch.

SPINAL TWIST

Muscles stretched: hip abductors (gluteus medius), obliques, lower back

Description: Keep the right leg straight, place the left foot on the outside of the right knee, place the right elbow against the outside of the left knee and look to the left as far as possible. Repeat the stretch for the other side of the body.

Performance Points:
• This exercise may also be performed laying supine (by keeping the shoulders flat on the ground and crossing one leg over the body).

QUAD STRETCH

Muscles stretched: quadriceps, iliopsoas, abdominals

Description: Lay on the right side, grab the left instep with the left hand and pull the heel toward the buttocks. Repeat the stretch for the right side of the body.

Performance Points:
• This movement may also be performed laying prone.

KNEE PULL

Muscles stretched: buttocks, hamstrings, lower back

Description: Lay supine on the ground with the legs extended. Grasp the left leg behind the knee and pull it toward the chest. Keep the right leg straight and the toes pointed upward. Repeat the stretch for the right side of the body.

Performance Points:
 • Using the arms to pull the leg toward the chest will permit a better stretch.

III. CONDITIONING FOR A PURPOSE

Most sports and activities require a combination of muscular strength and aerobic conditioning. A youth who is highly conditioned will have a lower resting heart rate and lower blood pressure. In addition, a highly conditioned youth will be able to work at higher levels of intensity for longer periods of time at a lower heart rate than someone who is less conditioned. This "conditioning advantage" means that a youth who competes in athletics won't have to expend as much energy as an opponent and will be able to perform activities with less visible effort. As conditioning improves, the heart rate will recover faster from exercise and return to its resting level more quickly. Finally, aerobic training — performed in conjunction with wise nutritional planning — will help maintain a youth's percentage of body fat and/or bodyweight at acceptable levels.

The Ultimate "Pump"

Aerobic conditioning can be improved by targeting the most important muscle in the body: the heart. Located just behind the sternum (or breastbone), the heart is the focal point of the aerobic system.

The heart is the ultimate endurance muscle or "pump" — it contracts about 100,000 times each day, pausing only briefly after a contraction to fill with more blood for its next contraction. Each half of the heart consists of two chambers: an atrium and a ventricle. The left half of the heart pumps blood to the body tissues, such as the skeletal muscles; the right half of the heart sends blood to the lungs. As the blood surges out of the ventricle, it pounds the arterial wall. This impact is transmitted along the length of the artery and can be felt as a throb or a "pulse" at those points where an artery lies just under the skin. The beat of the pulse is synchronous with the beat of the heart.

The Training Effect

Like other muscle tissue, the heart will hypertrophy — or get larger — from exercise. Specifically, its ventricular wall becomes thicker from anaerobic exercise (e.g., strength training) and its ventricular cavity becomes larger from aerobic exercise. This permits the heart to accept more blood and expel it more powerfully. As the heart becomes a better conditioned muscle, its ability to circulate blood also improves. In particular, the amount of blood pumped by the heart during each beat increases. As noted previously, the resting heart rate decreases as a direct result of aerobic conditioning. A slower heart rate coupled with the ejection of a larger volume of blood per beat indicates an efficient circulatory system.

Because of this training effect, athletes usually have a lower resting heart rate than sedentary individuals; in fact, some highly conditioned athletes have resting heart rates of less than 40 beats per minute (bpm). A lower resting heart rate may be especially important if the heart is limited to a certain number of beats over the course of a lifetime. For example, suppose that the human heart is confined to about 2.5 million beats before it simply wears out from the labors of continual usage. In this scenario, a person with an average resting heart rate of 60 bpm could expect to live a little more than 79 years; on the other hand, a person with an average resting heart rate of 70 bpm could expect to live a little less than 68 years. If this concept were true, a decrease in the resting heart rate of just 10 bpm would translate into more than 11 additional years of life. While this notion is intriguing, it has yet to have been proven scientifically. Nevertheless, it does generate the possibility of added importance in having a lower resting heart rate.

Aerobic Guidelines

A youth's aerobic fitness may be developed and improved by using several easy-to-follow guidelines. These guidelines have been developed by the American College of Sports Medicine

(ACSM) based upon the existing scientific evidence concerning exercise prescription and can be organized under the acronym FITT, which stands for Frequency, Intensity, Time and Type.

Frequency

In order to improve aerobic fitness, most authorities suggest that a selected activity should be performed 3-5 days per week. Exercising less than two days per week does not appear adequate enough to promote any meaningful changes in aerobic capacity. The amount of aerobic improvement from exercising more than five days per week is negligible.

Beginning with too much exercise too soon may very well lead to an overuse injury. Of specific concern is the potential for damage to the growth plates. To lessen the risk of overuse injury, younger and physically immature teens should perform an aerobic workout 2-3 times per week. As the teen develops physically, aerobic activities can be increased to 3-5 days per week.

Intensity

The most important component of an aerobic conditioning program is the level of intensity or effort. The heart rate increases in direct proportion to the intensity of the exercise. As such, the heart rate is commonly used as an estimate of aerobic intensity.

Since there is a slight but steady decrease in the maximal heart rate with aging, estimates of the maximal heart rate are made on the basis of age. The ACSM suggests that a level of 60-90 percent of the age-predicted maximum heart rate must be maintained to produce a desirable training effect. To find a rough estimate of the age-predicted maximum heart rate, simply subtract the age from 220. For example, the age-predicted maximum heart rate of a 15-year-old youth is 205 bpm [220 - 15 = 205]. To find the recommended heart rate training zone, multiply 205 bpm by .60 and .90. This means that a 15-year-old youth needs to maintain an exercise heart rate between about 123-185 bpm to elicit an aerobic conditioning effect [205 bpm x .60 = 123 bpm; 205 bpm x .90 = 184.5 bpm].

Older teens and physically mature teens as well as youths with above-average fitness levels will need to exercise at a higher percentage of their age-predicted maximum heart rate to receive a sufficient workload. On the other hand, younger and physically immature teens along with youths having a relatively low level of fitness should exercise closer to 60 percent of their age-predicted maximum heart rate or perhaps slightly lower. Exercising at a lower intensity should also be done in the early stages of a conditioning program. Remember, a favorable training response depends upon exercising with a high level of intensity or effort. For some youths, training with a lower percentage of their age-predicted maximum heart rate may actually represent a high level of intensity and an adequate workload for them.

The heart rate can be easily measured at several different sites on the body. There are numerous heart rate monitors that are available commercially that will give a reasonably accurate reading of the heart rate. However, the easiest and least expensive way is for youths to measure their own heart rate. This can be done by locating the pulse at either the carotid artery (in the neck) or the radial artery (in the wrist). Simply place the tips of the index and middle fingers over one of these sites. (During intense exercise, the carotid and the radial arteries will be easy to find.) Counting the pulse for 10 (or 15) seconds immediately after a conditioning session and multiplying that number by 6 (or 4) gives a good estimate of the exercise heart rate for one minute.

Time
In order for youths to improve their aerobic fitness, they must exercise continuously for 20-30 minutes. Again, performing too much exercise too soon may very well lead to an overuse injury. To lessen this risk, younger and physically immature teens should perform an aerobic workout for 15-20 minutes. A youth with a particularly low level of fitness will be more suited to an aerobic workout of even shorter duration — perhaps 5-10 minutes. As conditioning improves, the length of the conditioning session can be gradually increased. The duration of the conditioning workout can also be increased as a youth matures physically.

A variety of endurance activities may be used by youths to produce an aerobic conditioning effect.

Type

If the frequency, the intensity and the duration of the aerobic conditioning program are similar, (i.e., in terms of total caloric expenditure), training adaptations appear to be independent of the mode of aerobic activity. Therefore, a variety of endurance activities may be used by youths to obtain an aerobic conditioning effect. The preferred types of aerobic activities are those that require a continuous effort, are rhythmic in nature and involve large amounts of muscle mass. Traditional outdoor aerobic activities that can be used to meet these criteria include hiking, walking, jogging, running, cycling, cross country skiing, roller/in-line skating and rowing; popular indoor activities are aerobic dancing, swimming, ice skating, rope jumping and performing stationary exercises on specialized equipment such as rowers, cycles (upright or recumbent), motorized treadmills and steppers/stairclimbers. It should be noted that most of these aerobic options are recreational activities that can be performed — and enjoyed — throughout a lifetime.

Each aerobic modality has its strong and weak points. An activity like swimming is desirable because it's non-weightbearing — there's no stress on the body's joint structures. On the other hand, swimming requires a certain degree of proficiency. The exercising heart rate of youths with poor swimming skills may exceed their recommended heart rate training zone in a struggle just to stay afloat. Therefore, swimming would not be a good aerobic choice for a youth with poor swimming fundamentals. However, swimming is an excellent choice when skills are adequate.

In addition, some activities are not prudent for some youths who may be prone to injury or those who are likely to complicate an existing condition. For instance, rope jumping is a high impact activity associated with significantly more debilitating injuries than low impact and non-weightbearing activities. As such, rope jumping would not be recommended for a larger than average youth (larger due to either fat tissue or muscle tissue) because of the excessive stress on the ankles, the knees and the lower back. Furthermore, a youth with chronic low back pain would be more comfortable cycling in a recumbent position instead of in the traditional upright position to decrease the stress on the lumbar spine. So, the best advice is for youths to select suitable activities that are enjoyable, compatible with their skill levels and orthopedically safe.

To avoid boredom, it's important for youths to change modalities from time to time. Fortunately, aerobic training permits a large amount of variety in terms of exercise selection. As long as it's appropriate, the modality chosen to strengthen the heart is not as critical as the intensity and the duration of the activity. The heart doesn't know if a recumbent bike was used one day and a stairclimber the next.

Meaningful Exercise

Throughout the course of an aerobic conditioning program, the heart will gradually adapt to the demands placed on it. Over a period of time, the same workout — which was originally difficult for a youth — can be performed at a lower exercising heart rate. Also, the ability to maintain a higher training heart rate will become easier. As such, it's important to note that aerobic training needs to be progressively more challenging in order for a youth to make further improvements. For this reason, it's meaningful to keep accurate records of conditioning workouts in order to monitor the key program components — such as the duration of the workouts, the frequency of the training and the intensity levels (i.e., the exercise heart rate).

In a nutshell, a youth should perform aerobic exercise at a frequency, intensity and duration that are developmentally appropriate while using suitable activities that require a sustained effort. Remember, all of these guidelines must be included in a program in order to strengthen the heart and improve aerobic conditioning.

Scheduling Training Sessions

Essentially, there are two options for scheduling strength training and aerobic conditioning sessions: Both sessions can be performed on the same day or the sessions can be performed on alternate days. The advantage of doing both activities on the same day is that it permits a more complete recovery. If strength training is performed on one day and conditioning the next, the muscles will be constantly stressed and the body may not have adequate time to recover properly. After a while, it may also be very difficult for a youth to exercise several days in a row without a break while maintaining a high degree of enthusiasm and an appropriate level of intensity. Therefore, the recommended way of scheduling strength training and aerobic conditioning sessions is to do both activities on the same day. However, the activities may be done on alternating days if enough time is not available to perform both activities on the same day.

Sequence Of Activities

If skill work, conditioning and strength training are performed by a young athlete on the same day, better results will be obtained if the skill work is done first. Of all three activities, the one that is most important to an athlete is skill development. If youths are exhausted after conditioning and strength training, they'll be drained both physically and mentally. Therefore, they won't practice very hard or work on their technique very well. In fact, they're sure to be inattentive and their performance will probably be quite careless, labored and awkward. Furthermore, a youth is more prone to injury when practicing in a pre-fatigued state. Because of this, it's best not to practice athletic skills after strength training and/or conditioning activities.

Whether strength training or conditioning follows skill training depends upon the nature of the sport. If a sport or activity has a greater strength component (e.g., football and high jumping), then the strength training workout should come before the conditioning workout. On the other hand, if a sport or activity has a greater endurance component (e.g., basketball and soccer), then the conditioning workout should precede the strength workout. If overall fitness is the main objective, research indicates that better overall results are obtained when aerobic conditioning activities are performed before strength training activities.

Assessing Aerobic Fitness

There are a number of ways to accurately measure aerobic fitness in a laboratory. One way is to step up and down from a bench of a standard height at a fixed rate of stepping. Another way is to pedal a bicycle ergometer in an upright or a recumbent position using the legs and/or the arms. Perhaps the most widely used laboratory device is the motor-driven treadmill. Each of these devices makes it possible for an individual to exercise at different levels of intensity while maintaining the body in a relatively stable position. This allows a person to be instrumented to measure various physiological responses. For example, expired air can be collected to determine the exact amount of oxygen being consumed as well as the response of the heart rate, the blood pressure and the body temperature.

Laboratory testing is an excellent means of providing accurate and valid data. However, such tests can be expensive, time-consuming and impractical for most youths. A much more practical way of assessing aerobic fitness in a non-laboratory setting is to have youths perform a walking/running test or a running test. Two of the most widely used performance-based tests for evaluating aerobic fitness are the 12-Minute Walking/Running Test and the 1.5-Mile Running Test. (A 1-Mile Running Test can be used for younger and physically immature teens.) The primary objective of the 12-Minute Walking/Running Test is to cover the greatest amount of distance in the allotted time period; in the case of the 1.5-Mile (or 1-Mile) Running Test, the youth attempts to run the distance in the least amount of time.

Table 3.1 lists normative data for various distances covered (in miles) during the 12-Minute Walking/Running Test for 13- to 19-year-olds. For example, a young boy who covered 1.75 miles in 12 minutes would be assessed as "excellent." Table 3.2 shows normative data for various times (in minutes and seconds) during the 1.5-Mile Running Test for 13-19 year olds. For instance, a young girl who ran 1.5 miles in 11:30 (11 minutes and 30 seconds) would have a "superior" level of aerobic fitness. (Note that both tests should be performed on a track or other level surface of known distance.)

Finally, the purpose of assessing aerobic fitness should not be to compare the performance of one youth to another. It's unfair to make comparisons between youths because each person has a different genetic potential for achieving aerobic fitness. Fitness assessments are more meaningful and fair when a youth's performance is compared to his or her last performance — not to the performance of others.

FITNESS	MALE	FEMALE
Superior	> 1.87	> 1.52
Excellent	1.73 — 1.86	1.44 — 1.51
Good	1.57 — 1.72	1.30 — 1.43
Fair	1.38 — 1.56	1.19 — 1.29
Poor	1.30 — 1.37	1.00 — 1.18
Very Poor	<1.30	< 1.00

TABLE 3.1: Normative data for 12-minute walk/run for 13- to 19-year-olds in miles. (Source: Cooper, K.H. 1982. *The aerobic program for total well-being*. New York, NY: M. Evans & Co.)

FITNESS	MALE	FEMALE
Superior	< 8:37	< 11:50
Excellent	8:37 — 9:40	11:50 — 12:29
Good	9:41 — 10:48	12:30 — 14:30
Fair	10:49 — 12:10	14:31 — 16:54
Poor	12:11 — 15:30	16:55 — 18:30
Very Poor	> 15:31	> 18:31

TABLE 3.2: Normative data for 1.5-mile run for 13- to 19-year-olds in minutes. (Source: Cooper, K. H. 1982. *The aerobic program for total well-being.* New York, NY: M. Evans & Co.)

IV. INCREASING FUNCTIONAL STRENGTH

The primary purpose of strength training by athletes is to decrease their injury potential and its second purpose is to increase their performance potential. Make no mistake about it — strength training is primarily a mechanism to prevent injury. Increasing the strength of the muscles, bones and connective tissue will reduce the likelihood that young athletes will incur an injury. That doesn't mean that a youth will never get hurt . . . sometimes injuries are a matter of being in the wrong spot at the wrong time. However, strength training will reduce that risk considerably. And, young athletes who improve their functional strength will be taking an important step in realizing their physical potential.

Physical Maturation

Determining the earliest age at which a youth can safely initiate a strength training program is based upon skeletal development. Chronologically, a youth might be 13 years old but may only be 11 in terms of skeletal maturation; conversely, another 13 year old might possess the skeleton of a 15 year old. These wide individual variations in physical maturation can create a difficult dilemma for establishing a reasonably safe age at which to begin strength training. Skeletal age can be predicted accurately from the X rays of bones in various parts of the body such as the hand and the wrist. However, physicians sometimes use assessments that are more practical. For example, the Tanner Staging System is used to predict strength, muscle and epiphyseal maturity by using various stages of the development of the secondary sexual characteristics such as the pubic hair, genitalia, breasts (in females) and plasma hormone levels.

The adolescent growth spurt is a period of accelerated increases in height and weight that occurs with the onset of adolescence. The age of onset and the duration of the spurt varies considerably from one individual to another. The adolescent growth spurt usually accompanies the onset of sexual maturation. In normal boys, the adolescent growth spurt may begin as early as the age of 10-1/2 or a late as 16. For the average boy, rapid acceleration in growth begins at about 13 years of age. In normal girls, the adolescent growth spurt may begin as early as 7-1/2 years of age or as late as 14-1/2. For the average girl, rapid acceleration in growth begins at about 11 years of age.

Unfortunately, there is no clear-cut borderline for determining a safe age at which to begin strength training because each person "ages" at a different rate. However, most youths are physically mature enough to begin strength training at about the age of 13 or 14.

Strength Training Guidelines

Science has been unable to discover one strength training method that is superior to another. Research has only shown that there are a variety of training methods using different combinations of sets and repetitions that will increase strength. Since just about any type of program will yield favorable results, a decision must be made as to what is most practical for youths based upon safety and time considerations.

A safe, efficient, productive, comprehensive and practical workout for youths can be performed with virtually any type of equipment by using the following ten principles of strength development:

1. Train with an appropriate level of intensity.
The intensity of effort is the most important controllable factor in determining a youth's response from strength training. Essentially, the harder youths train, the better their response. In the weight room, an appropriate level of intensity is characterized by performing each exercise to the point of muscular failure: when the muscles have been exhausted such that no additional repetitions can be performed. Failure to reach a desirable level

of intensity — or muscular fatigue — will result in little or no gains in muscular size or strength. Simply, a submaximal effort will yield submaximal results. (Intensity should not be confused with a percentage of maximum weight.)

The Overload Principle states that in order to increase muscular size and strength, a muscle must be stressed — or "overloaded" — with a workload that is beyond its present capacity. The intensity of effort must be great enough to exceed this "threshold" level so that a sufficient amount of muscular fatigue is produced to trigger an adaptive response: muscular growth. Given proper nourishment and an adequate amount of recovery between workouts, a muscle will adapt to these demands by increasing in size and strength.

Younger teens may not be comfortable training to the point of muscular fatigue. Youths who aren't comfortable with this level of intensity can terminate the exercise a few repetitions short of muscular failure. As the teen develops physically, the intensity can be gradually increased.

Older and physically mature teens can increase the intensity of the exercise by performing 3-5 additional post-fatigue repetitions after reaching muscular failure. The 2 most popular types of post-fatigue repetitions are negatives and regressions. These intensification repetitions will allow the muscles to be overloaded in a safe, efficient manner. (It should be noted that post-fatigue repetitions should be used carefully and infrequently and only with physically mature teens.)

When you reach a point where you are unable to raise the weight (i.e., muscular failure), you still have the ability to lower the weight. To perform "negatives," a training partner raises the weight and the lifter lowers the weight. This is repeated for 3-5 repetitions with each negative repetition lasting about 6-8 seconds. As an example, suppose that a youth reached muscular failure on a leg extension. A partner would help the youth raise the weight until the lifter's legs are extended. Then, the lifter lowers the weight under control back to the starting/stretched position.

To perform regressions (also called "breakdowns" or "burnouts"), a youth (or a training partner) would quickly reduce the starting weight by about 25-30 percent (after reaching muscular failure) and do 3-5 post-fatigue repetitions with the lighter resistance. For instance, let's say a youth did 15 repetitions with 50 pounds on the calf raise before reaching muscular failure. The youth (or training partner) would immediately reduce the weight to about 35-40 pounds and would then attempt to perform 3-5 repetitions with the lighter weight. If desired, a second series of 3-5 regressions may be performed immediately after the first series by reducing the lightened load by 25-30 percent. (In this example, the 35-40 pounds would be quickly reduced to about 25-30 pounds.)

2. Attempt to increase the resistance used or the repetitions performed every workout.

Unfortunately, little of what is done in most weight rooms can be characterized as being "progressive." It's not uncommon to hear of someone who performs the same number of repetitions with the same amount of weight over and over again, workout after workout. Suppose that today you did a set of leg curls for 10 repetitions with 50 pounds and a month later you're still doing 10 repetitions with 50 pounds. Did you increase your strength? Probably not. On the other hand, what if you were able to do 11 repetitions with 60 pounds a month later? In this case, you were able to perform 10 percent more repetitions with 20 percent more weight — excellent progress over a period of one month.

If a muscle is to continually increase in size and strength it must be forced to do progressively harder work. The muscles must be overloaded with a workload that is increased steadily and systematically throughout the course of a strength training program. In order to overload the muscles, youths must attempt to increase either the weight they use or the repetitions they perform in relation to their previous workout.

When the maximum number of prescribed repetitions are attained, the resistance should be increased for the next workout. Progressions should not be in huge increments . . . but the weight must always be challenging. The resistance should be increased in an amount that a youth is comfortable with. Generally, the muscles will respond better if the progressions in resistance are

Increasing the strength of the muscles, bones and connective tissue will reduce the likelihood that young athletes will incur an injury. (photo by Christine Russell)

Strength training will be safer and more efficient when youths perform each repetition with proper technique.

five percent or less. But again, the resistance must always be challenging. If a youth is just beginning a strength training program, or the exercises in a routine are changed, it may take several workouts before a challenging weight is found. That's okay — the youth should simply continue to make progressions in the resistance as needed.

Everyone has a different potential for developing strength. As such, the amount of weight a youth can lift shouldn't be compared to that of anyone else. Youths should only be compared to what they can lift relative to their previous performances.

3. Perform one set of each exercise to the point of muscular fatigue.

If performed properly, traditional multiple-set routines (i.e., more than one set) can be effective in overloading a muscle. They've been used successfully by competitive weightlifters and bodybuilders for decades. And, since many strength and fitness professionals have competed in weightlifting meets and bodybuilding events, it's no surprise that most athletic and recreational programs incorporate a traditional multiple-set program.

In seeking the most practical and time-efficient strength training method possible, a necessary question is: Can performing one set of each exercise with a desirable level of intensity produce the same results as performing two or three sets? The answer is a resounding yes. Recall that in order for a muscle to increase in size and strength, it must be fatigued or overloaded. It's that simple. It really doesn't matter whether the muscles are fatigued in one set or several sets — as long as the muscles experience a certain level of exhaustion. An overwhelming amount of research has shown that doing one set of each exercise produces significant strength improvements and is comparable to doing multiple sets. In addition, performing one set to muscular failure is a popular method of strength training that has been advocated by numerous strength and fitness authorities. Of course, if a single set of an exercise is to be productive, the set must be done with an appropriate level of intensity (i.e., to the point of muscular failure). The muscle(s) must be completely fatigued at the end of each exercise.

If doing one set of an exercise is productive and produces similar results as two or three sets, then a one-set protocol represents a more efficient and practical means of strength training. After all, why perform several sets when comparable results can be obtained from one set in a fraction of the time? Again, this is not to say that traditional multiple-set programs are unproductive. It's just that multiple sets are extremely inefficient in terms of time and, therefore, are undesirable. Performing too many sets can also create a situation in which the muscles are broken down in such an extreme manner that it restricts muscular growth. Finally, doing multiple sets can significantly increase the risk of incurring an overuse injury — such as tendinitis — due to repetitive muscular trauma.

The quality of work done in the weight room should be emphasized rather than the quantity of work. Meaningless sets should not be performed — every single exercise should count. The most efficient program is one that produces the maximum possible results in the least amount of time.

4. Reach muscular failure within a developmentally appropriate number of repetitions.

Older and physically mature teens should reach muscular failure within 15-20 repetitions for exercises involving their hips, 10-15 repetitions for their legs and 6-12 repetitions for their upper torso. Younger and physically immature teens should use slightly higher repetition ranges — such as 20-25 repetitions for exercises involving their hips, 15-20 repetitions for their legs and 10-15 repetitions for their upper torso. The higher repetition ranges will necessitate using somewhat lighter weights, which will in turn reduce the stress placed upon their bones and joints.

If muscular failure occurs before the lower level of the repetition range is reached, the weight is too heavy and should be reduced for the next workout. If the upper level of the repetition range is exceeded before muscular failure is experienced, the weight is too light and should be increased for the next workout by five percent or less.

It should be noted that performing low-repetition movements that are considerably less than recommended will increase the risk of injury. Likewise, as an exercise exceeds the recommended repetition ranges, it becomes a greater test of aerobic endurance rather than muscular strength.

5. Perform each repetition with proper technique.

A repetition consists of raising the weight to the mid-range position, pausing briefly and then returning the weight to the starting/stretched position. A repetition is also performed over the greatest possible range of motion that safety permits.

Youths should raise the weight in a deliberate, controlled manner without any jerking movements. Lifting a weight in a rapid, explosive fashion is ill-advised for two reasons: (1) it introduces momentum into the movement which makes the exercise less productive and less efficient and (2) it exposes the muscles, joint structures and connective tissue to potentially dangerous forces which magnify the likelihood of incurring an injury while strength training. Lifting a weight in about 1-2 seconds guarantees that a youth is exercising in a safe, efficient manner.

After raising the weight, a youth should pause briefly in the position of full muscle contraction or the "mid-range" position. Most individuals are very weak in the mid-range of exercises because they rarely, if ever, emphasize that position. Pausing momentarily in this position allows youths to focus attention on their muscles when they are fully contracted. Further, a brief pause in the mid-range position permits a smooth transition between the raising and the lowering of the weight and helps eliminate the effects of momentum. If a youth cannot pause momentarily in the mid-range position, then the weight was moved too quickly and thrown into position.

Research and applications have shown that individuals can always lower more weight than they can raise. Because of this, the lowering portion of the movement should be emphasized for a longer time. It should take about 3-4 seconds to lower the weight back to the starting/stretched position. The lowering of the weight should also be emphasized because it makes the exercise more efficient: The same muscles that are used to raise the weight are also used to lower it. By emphasizing the lowering of a weight, each repetition becomes more efficient and each set becomes more productive. Lowering the weight in a controlled manner also ensures that the exercised muscle is being stretched properly and safely.

In effect, each repetition would be roughly 4-6 seconds in length. Most strength and fitness professionals who are opposed to explosive, ballistic movements in the weight room consider a 4-6 second repetition as a general guideline for lifting "under control" or "without momentum."

Finally, a quality repetition is done throughout the greatest possible range of motion that safety allows — from a position of full stretch to a position of full muscular contraction and back to a position of full stretch. Exercising throughout a full range of motion allows youths to maintain (or perhaps increase) their flexibility, which reduces their potential for injury. Furthermore, it ensures that the entire muscle is being exercised — not just a portion of it — thereby making the movement more efficient. In general, full-range exercise is necessary for a full-range effect.

Remember, how youths lift a weight is more important than how much weight they lift. Strength training will be safer and more efficient when youths perform each repetition with proper technique.

6. Strength train for no more than 40 minutes per workout.

More isn't necessarily better when it comes to strength training. It is important to understand that an inverse relationship exists between time and intensity: As the time or the length of an activity increases, the level of intensity decreases. The fact is a youth can exercise for a short period of time with a high level of intensity or a long period of time with an low level of intensity. However, a youth cannot possibly train at an appropriate level of intensity for a long period of time. In order to train with a desirable level of intensity, a youth must train for a relatively brief period of time. It should be noted that increasing the number of sets or exercises performed will increase the length of time a youth is exercising and decrease the level of intensity.

Under normal circumstances, a youth who spends much more than 40 minutes in the weight room is probably not training with an appropriate level of intensity. A productive workout for older and physically mature teens can be performed in 30-40 minutes. Younger and physically immature teens should limit their workout to 20-30 minutes. Youths do not need to spend much more time than that engaged in strength training activities. The risk of overuse injuries will be greatly reduced by eliminating marathon strength sessions in the weight room.

The transition time between one exercise and another will vary with a youth's level of conditioning. Youths can proceed from one exercise to the next as soon as they "catch their breath" or feel that they are able to produce a maximal level of effort. After an initial period of adjustment, adequate recovery should occur within 1-3 minutes.

7. Perform no more than about 14 exercises each workout.

For most older and physically mature teens, a complete strength training program can be performed using 14 exercises or less during each workout. Younger and physically immature teens should perform about 9 exercises or less. This lower volume of exercises decreases the potential for overuse injury.

For older and physically mature teens, one exercise should be done for their hips, hamstrings, quadriceps, calves/dorsi flexors, biceps, triceps, abdominals and lower back. Two exercises should be selected for their chest, upper back (the "lats") and shoulders. Younger and physically immature teens should perform one exercise for their hips, hamstrings, quadriceps, calves/dorsi flexors, chest, upper back, shoulders, abdominals and lower back. Youths should select any exercises they prefer in order to train those bodyparts.

For some youths, a thorough workout may require slightly more movements. For instance, a comprehensive workout for a youth who is involved in a combative sport — such as football, wrestling or judo — must include an additional 2-4 neck exercises to strengthen and protect the cervical area against possible traumatic injury. Additionally, a youth involved in a sport or activity that requires grip strength — such as baseball or tennis — should perform one forearm exercise.

Once again, more isn't necessarily better when it comes to strength training. Performing too many exercises may produce too much muscular fatigue which will not permit muscular growth — and may even produce a loss in muscle size and strength. In addition, the more exercises that are performed, the harder it will be to maintain a desirable level of intensity. Remember, a large amount of low-intensity exercise will do very little in the way of increasing strength.

Occasionally, an extra movement may be performed to emphasize a particular bodypart. However, if a youth starts to level off or "plateau" in one or more exercises, it's probably from doing too many movements.

8. Whenever possible, exercise the muscles from largest to smallest.

A strength training program should begin with exercises that influence the largest muscles and proceed to those that involve the smallest muscles. Exercises for the hips should be performed first, followed by the upper legs (hamstrings and quadriceps), the lower legs (calves or dorsi flexors), the upper torso (chest, upper back and shoulders), the arms (biceps, triceps and forearms), the abdominals and finally the lower back.

It is important to note that the mid-section should not be fatigued early in the workout. The abdominals stabilize the rib cage and aid in forced expiration. Therefore, early fatigue of the abdominals would detract from the performance of the other exercises that involve larger, more powerful muscles. The low back should be the very last muscle to be exercised. Fatiguing the low back earlier in the workout will also hinder the performance of other movements.

The neck can be exercised at the beginning of the workout or just after the lower body (prior to beginning the upper body movements). This would seem to violate the "largest to smallest" rule. However, youths will be fatigued both physically and mentally at the end of a workout. Because of this, they're less likely to train the all-important neck area with a desirable level of effort or enthusiasm. Exercising the neck earlier in a workout when a youth is not fatigued elicits a more favorable response.

It is especially important not to exercise the arms before exercising the upper torso or to exercise the legs before exercising the hips. Multiple-joint movements require the use of smaller, weaker muscles to assist in the exercise. (As a rule of thumb, the arms are the weak link when performing multiple-joint movements for the upper body and the legs are the weak link when performing multiple-joint movements for the hips.) If the smaller muscles are fatigued first, an already weak link will be weakened further, thereby limiting the workload placed on the larger, more powerful muscles and will restrict the potential for their development. As such, the smaller muscles should not be exercised before the larger muscles.

9. Strength train no more than 3 times per week on nonconsecutive days.

Muscles do not get stronger during a workout — muscles get stronger during the recovery from a workout. When weights are lifted, muscle tissue is broken down and the recovery process allows the muscle time to rebuild itself. Think of this as allowing a wound to heal. If you had a scab and picked at it every day, you would delay the healing process, but if you left it alone you would permit the damaged tissue time to heal. There are individual variations in recovery ability — everyone has different levels of tolerance for exercise. However, a period of about 48-72 hours is usually necessary for muscle tissue to recover sufficiently from a strength workout. As such, it is suggested that strength training be performed on nonconsecutive days — such as on Monday, Wednesday and Friday.

To lessen the risk of overuse injury, younger and physically immature teens should strength train 1-2 times per week. As the teen matures physically, strength training can be increased to 2-3 days per week. Strength training places great demands and stress on the muscles. Performing any more than three sessions a week will gradually become counterproductive if the demands placed on the muscles exceed their recovery ability.

How do you know if a youth has had sufficient recovery time? There should be a gradual improvement in the amount of weight and/or the number of repetitions that a youth is able to do over the course of several weeks. If not, then the youth is probably not getting enough of a recovery between workouts.

Athletes are encouraged to continue strength training even while in-season or while competing to maintain (or improve) their strength throughout the season. However, the frequency of workouts should be reduced due to the increased activity level of practices and competitions. If two weekly workouts are performed, one session should be done as soon as possible following a competition and another no later than 48 hours before the next competition. So, a youth who competes on Saturdays and Tuesdays should strength train on Sundays and Wednesdays (or Thursdays — providing that it's not within 48 hours of the next competition). From time to time, a youth may only be able to strength train once a week because of a particularly heavy schedule (e.g., competing three times in one week).

10. Keep accurate records of performance.
The importance of accurate record keeping cannot be overemphasized. Records are a log of what a youth has accomplished during each and every exercise of each and every strength session. In a sense, a workout card is a history of the activities in the weight room.

A workout card is an extremely valuable tool for youths to monitor their progress and make their workouts more meaningful. It can also be used to identify exercises in which they've reached a plateau. In the unfortunate event of an injury, the effectiveness of the rehabilitative process can be gauged if there is a record of the pre-injury strength levels.

A workout card can take an infinite number of appearances. However, youths should be able to record their bodyweight, the date of each workout, the weight used for each exercise, the number of repetitions performed for each exercise, the order in which the exercises were completed and any necessary seat adjustments.

In addition, it's helpful to separate the exercises according to bodyparts along with the suggested number of exercises that are to be performed for each bodypart. The card can list specific exercises and the more common movements (e.g., leg curl, leg extension, bench press) and/or may contain blank spaces so youths can fill in their own menu of exercises. The recommended repetition ranges should also be given for each exercise along with spaces to record any seat adjustments. A sample workout card is shown in Figure 4.2.

The area to the immediate right of this information is where the data can be recorded from the strength training sessions. Figure 4.1 details how to record the weight used, the repetitions performed and the order in which the exercises were completed.

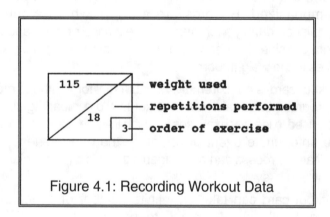

Figure 4.1: Recording Workout Data

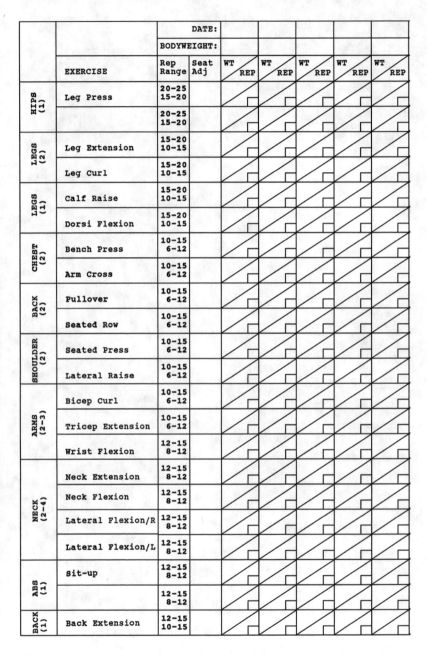

	EXERCISE	Rep Range	Seat Adj	WT / REP	WT / REP	WT / REP	WT / REP	WT / REP
HIPS (1)	Leg Press	20-25 15-20						
		20-25 15-20						
LEGS (2)	Leg Extension	15-20 10-15						
	Leg Curl	15-20 10-15						
LEGS (1)	Calf Raise	15-20 10-15						
	Dorsi Flexion	15-20 10-15						
CHEST (2)	Bench Press	10-15 6-12						
	Arm Cross	10-15 6-12						
BACK (2)	Pullover	10-15 6-12						
	Seated Row	10-15 6-12						
SHOULDER (2)	Seated Press	10-15 6-12						
	Lateral Raise	10-15 6-12						
ARMS (2-3)	Bicep Curl	10-15 6-12						
	Tricep Extension	10-15 6-12						
	Wrist Flexion	12-15 8-12						
NECK (2-4)	Neck Extension	12-15 8-12						
	Neck Flexion	12-15 8-12						
	Lateral Flexion/R	12-15 8-12						
	Lateral Flexion/L	12-15 8-12						
ABS (1)	Sit-up	12-15 8-12						
		12-15 8-12						
BACK (1)	Back Extension	12-15 10-15						

Figure 4.2: Sample Workout Card (Note: Appropriate repetition ranges and volume of exercises should be used.)

The risk of overuse injuries will be greatly reduced by eliminating marathon strength sessions in the weight room.

V. DESIGNING AND REVISING THE STRENGTH TRAINING PROGRAM

A strength training program should be geared toward each youth's likes and dislikes in terms of exercise selection and equipment preference. This chapter will describe how to effectively structure and fine-tune a personalized program using the ten strength training principles detailed in Chapter 4 in conjunction with the exercises that will be described in Chapters 7 through 14.

Overview Of Program Design

A practical and time-efficient program can be performed using no more than about 14 exercises during each workout (younger and physically immature teens should perform about 9 exercises or less). Youths who participate in combative sports should perform an additional 2-4 neck exercises as a safeguard against cervical injury; others should do one forearm movement if increased grip strength is desired for a sport or activity.

Recall that it is best to exercise the muscles from largest to smallest: hips, upper legs (hamstrings and quadriceps), lower legs (calves or dorsi flexors), upper torso (chest, upper back and shoulders), arms (biceps, triceps and forearms), abdominals and lower back.

Antagonistic Muscles
Muscles are arranged in the body in opposing functions, such as flexors-extensors, abductors-adductors and so on. As an example, the biceps flex (or bend) the arm at the elbow and the triceps extend (or straighten) the arm at the elbow. When one muscle acts in opposition to another, it is referred to as an antagonist. In addition to the biceps-triceps pairing, other antagonistic partnerships include the hip abductors-hip adductors, hamstrings-quadriceps, calves-dorsi flexors, chest-upper back, anterior deltoid-posterior deltoid, forearm flexors-forearm extensors and abdominals-lower back.

A strength training program should not emphasize certain muscle groups without also addressing their antagonistic counterparts in some fashion. Too much emphasis on one bodypart may eventually produce abnormal development or create a muscle imbalance, which can predispose a youth to injury. For instance, too many chest exercises may lead to a round-shouldered appearance; too much work on the quadriceps may make a youth susceptible to a hamstring pull.

Types of Movements

Essentially, there are two types of exercise movements: single-joint and multiple-joint. A single-joint movement involves a range of motion around only one joint. The advantage of a single-joint movement is that it usually provides muscle isolation. A good example is a pullover, in which the upper arm rotates around the shoulder joint thereby isolating the upper back muscles.

A multiple-joint movement involves ranges of motion around more than one joint. For instance, during a lat pulldown, there is rotation around both the shoulder and the elbow joints — the upper back pulls the upper arm backward around the shoulder joint and the bicep bends the arm at the elbow joint. There's even some work being done at the wrist joint by the forearm flexors to maintain a grip on the bar. Multiple-joint exercises are advantageous because relatively large amounts of muscle mass can be worked in one movement.

Whenever two exercises are done for a particular bodypart (i.e., the chest, upper back and shoulders), one of the selections should be a multiple-joint movement and the other should be a single-joint movement. Why one of each?

Multiple-joint movements have a distinct disadvantage because they generally have a "weak link." When an individual fatigues in a multiple-joint exercise it's because the resistance has been filtered through a smaller, weaker muscle that exhausts well before the larger and stronger muscle has received a sufficient workload. In an exercise such as the aforementioned lat pulldown, the biceps are the smaller muscle and, therefore, will fatigue long before the upper back. In fact, the forearm muscles may fatigue even earlier than the biceps. So, the biceps and the forearms get an adequate workload but the upper back — which is really the target of the exercise — gets very little stimulus. Therefore, if two multiple-joint movements have been selected as the two exercise options for a particular bodypart, the smaller muscle structures will receive much of the workload and the larger muscles will receive very little.

On the one hand, a single-joint movement is superior to a multiple-joint movement because it allows a person to isolate a large muscle without being impaired by the limited strength capacity of a small muscle. On the other hand, a multiple-joint movement is superior to a single-joint movement because it exercises a larger amount of muscle mass. Therefore, both single-joint and multiple-joint movements have advantages and disadvantages. This doesn't mean that it would be totally wrong to do two multiple-joint movements for the same bodypart. However, a strength training routine will be more efficient and productive if a single-joint movement is selected to offset the limitations of a multiple-joint movement.

Exercise Options

A composite list of the exercises detailed in Chapters 7 through 14 appears in Figure 5.1. Free weights (i.e., barbells and dumbbells), machines (selectorized and plate-loading) and manual resistance are the featured exercises in these chapters. Naturally, the options will differ based upon the available equipment. It would be next to impossible to list exercises for every manufacturer's strength training machines. However, many companies market products that are quite similar to that shown in terms of design and function. Barbells and dumbbells are fairly standard and are usually available at most high schools and fitness centers. Finally, manual resistance exercises are always an option, provided that a partner is available.

Based on the information contained in this and the previous chapter, two sample workouts have been constructed and are shown in Figure 5.2. (One sample workout would be for older and physically mature teens; the other sample workout would be for younger and physically immature teens.) Note that the design of a strength training routine can have almost an infinite number of possibilities. The only limits are your available equipment and your imagination.

Overcoming The Strength "Plateau"

Periodically, a point will be reached in training where strength gains level off or "plateau. " Quite often, this is a result of overtraining — entirely too much work is being performed, which causes the muscular system to be overstressed. In effect, the demands of the activity have exceeded the youth's recovery ability. In this case, the volume of work being done in the weight room simply needs to be reduced.

It is important to understand that an athlete's strength gains will be minimal during the season, especially as practices become more intense. Although this isn't necessarily cause for alarm, the workout frequency and the total number of exercises that are performed in the weight room may need to be reduced to allow for adequate recovery. In any event, the added activity of practices, competitions and sometimes even traveling will make strength gains difficult to accomplish during the season.

Sometimes, however, a youth's strength will plateau as a result of performing the same workouts over and over again for lengthy periods of time. In these instances, the workout has become a form of unproductive manual labor that is monotonous, dull and unchallenging.

Monotony can be prevented by revising or varying the strength training workouts. As an example, a youth can do an entirely different workout during each of the three weekly sessions, such as Workout A on Monday, Workout B on Wednesday and Workout

---

Figure 5.1 Equipment Codes:

BB - Barbell, BW - Bodyweight, DB - Dumbbell,

MR - Manual Resistance, PM - Plate-loading Machine,

SM - Selectorized Machine

Bodypart	Exercise	Equipment
Hips	Leg Press Hip Abduction Hip Adduction	PM, SM MR, SM MR, SM
Upper Leg	Leg Curl Leg Extension	MR, PM, SM MR, PM, SM
Lower Leg	Calf Raise Dorsi Flexion	DB, PM, SM MR, PM, SM
Chest	Push-up Bench Press Incline Press Decline Press Dip Bent Arm Fly	BW, MR BB, DB, PM, SM BB, DB, PM, SM BB, DB, PM, SM BW, PM, SM DB, MR, PM, SM
Upper Back	Lat Pulldown Seated Row Bent Over Row Chin Pullover	MR, PM, SM MR, PM, SM DB, MR BW, PM, SM DB, PM, SM
Shoulders	Seated Press Lateral Raise Front Raise Bent Over Raise Internal Rotation External Rotation Upright Row Shoulder Shrug	BB, DB, MR, PM, SM DB, MR, PM, SM DB, MR DB, MR DB, MR, PM, SM DB, MR, PM, SM BB, DB, PM, SM BB, DB, PM, SM
Arms	Bicep Curl Tricep Extension	BB, DB, MR, PM, SM BB, DB, MR, PM, SM
Forearms	Wrist Flexion Wrist Extension	BB, DB, MR, PM, SM DB
Abdominals	Sit-up Side Bend Knee-up	BW, MR, PM, SM DB, SM BW, SM
Lower Back	Back Extension	BW, SM
Neck	Neck Extension Neck Flexion Lateral Flexion	MR, PM, SM MR, PM, SM MR, PM, SM

Figure 5.1: Composite List of Exercise Options

Sample Routine #1	Reps	Sample Routine #2	Reps
Leg Press (PM)	15 -20	Leg Press (SM)	20-25
Leg Curl (MR)	10 -15	Leg Curl (SM)	15-20
Leg Extension (SM)	10 -15	Leg Extension (PM)	15-20
Calf Raise (DB)	10 -15	Dorsi Flexion (MR)	15-20
Bench Press (BB)	6 -12	Push-up (BW)	10-15
Bent Arm Fly (MR)	6 -12	Lat Pulldown (SM)	10-15
Seated Row (SM)	6 -12	Upright Row (BB)	10-15
Pullover (SM)	6 -12	Sit-up (BW)	12-15
Seated Press (DB)	6 -12	Back Extension (BW)	15-20
Lateral Raise (MR)	6 -12		
Bicep Curl (BB)	6 -12		
Tricep Extension (SM)	6 -12		
Knee-up (BW)	8 -12		
Back Extension (SM)	10 -15		

Figure 5.2: Two Sample Routines
(Note: Sample Routine #1 would be for older and physically mature teens; Sample Routine #2 would be for younger and physically immature teens.)

Equipment Codes:

 BB - Barbell, BW - Bodyweight, DB - Dumbbell,
MR - Manual Resistance, PM - Plate-loading Machine,
SM - Selectorized Machine

C on Friday. Another possibility is to perform the same workout one week and a different one the next. Or, one or two aspects of the workout can simply be changed as needed in order to inject a little enthusiasm back into the strength training program.

Simply checking the workout card will reveal if a youth has begun to level off. The workout card should be reviewed carefully, however. If a youth appears to have reached a plateau in a certain movement, the performance in earlier exercises of that workout must be considered. For instance, suppose a youth did 15 repetitions with 60 pounds on the leg extension for five consecutive workouts. At first glance, it may not seem as if the youth's quadriceps have gotten any stronger. However, what if the youth's leg press increased from 150 pounds to 165 pounds during those same five workouts? That means the load on the youth's hips, hamstrings and quadriceps increased by 10 percent, or an average of 2 percent per workout. In other words, the youth's quadriceps were increasingly more pre-fatigued each time prior to performing leg extensions. In this case, there's little doubt that the youth's quadriceps did get stronger. In fact, simply being able to duplicate past performances on the leg extensions would actually be quite a feat, although that would not be readily apparent. Similarly, if the weight used in the bicep curl levels off, it's possible that increasingly heavier weights are being used by the biceps earlier in the workout — perhaps during lat pulldowns, seated rows or upright rows. So, the entire workout must be considered when determining whether a youth has indeed reached a plateau.

Youths won't be able to improve their performance in every exercise from one workout to the next. However, gradual strength gains should be observed in all exercises over the course of about four or five workouts. Failure to make a progression in an exercise (in resistance or in repetitions) by this time is a signal to change some aspect of the routine. There are several ways that this may be accomplished.

Rearrange the Order
One of the easiest ways to modify a workout is to rearrange the order in which the exercises for a particular bodypart are

performed. For example, a youth who has been doing an upright row followed by a seated press can simply switch these two movements so that the seated press is done first and the upright row next.

Whenever the order of exercises is varied, the weights that are used must be adjusted accordingly. Using the previous example, let's say 35 pounds is normally used in the upright row, followed quickly by a seated press using 45 pounds. If the order of the exercises is changed (i.e., the seated press is done first), the youth's shoulder musculature will be relatively fresh for the seated press and, therefore, would now be able to handle more resistance in that movement. However, the weight usually used in the upright row must be reduced since the youth's deltoids will be more fatigued than when the seated press is performed first.

An additional possibility is to exercise the muscle groups in a different sequence. Instead of going from chest to upper back to shoulders, a youth might start with the upper back exercises, proceed to the shoulder movements and then finish with the chest area. So, an upper torso routine of bench press, bent arm fly, lat pulldown, pullover, seated press and lateral raise could be changed to pullover, lat pulldown, lateral raise, seated press, bent arm fly and bench press. Once again, any time the sequence of exercises is rearranged, the levels of resistance will need to be adjusted accordingly.

Change the Modality
Another way to vary a workout is to change the modality or the equipment used. For instance, if a youth plateaus on the bench press, a similar movement can be done using different equipment. Chapter 9 describes several different ways of doing a bench press using a barbell, dumbbells, a selectorized machine and a plate-loading machine. Obviously, the extent to which the modality can be changed depends upon the equipment that is on hand.

Alternate the Exercises
A third means of varying a workout is to alternate the exercises that involve the same muscle group(s). For example, the bench press, incline press, decline press and dip are all multiple-joint

Youths who participate in combative sports — such as football or wrestling — should perform 2-4 neck exercises as a safeguard against cervical injury.

Monotony can be prevented by revising or varying the strength training workouts.

chest movements that also exercise the shoulders and the triceps. If a youth peaks in one of these exercises, another movement can simply be substituted that employs the same musculature. Once again, the availability of equipment will determine how much the exercises may be alternated.

Vary the Repetition

A final option is to vary the manner in which the repetitions are done. Repetitions are ordinarily performed in a bilateral manner — that is, with both limbs at the same time. Repetitions can be done at least three other ways: unilateral, modified cadence and extended pause.

Unilateral repetitions. As a variation in the repetition style, many exercises may be done unilaterally — that is, with one limb at a time. Exercising with unilateral movements would be especially recommended for a youth with a strength imbalance between one side of the body and the other. Unilateral movements are also advised for youths who experience an exaggerated rise in their blood pressure while strength training.

Modified cadence repetitions. The cadence of a repetition may be varied from the usual "up two, down four "(or simply 2/4) speed of movement. For example, the Super Slow protocol calls for each repetition to be raised in 10 seconds and lowered in 5 seconds (or 10/5). A 4/4 speed of movement has also been suggested as a safe, productive variation of the traditional 2/4 speed.

Extended pause repetitions. The importance of including a momentary pause in the mid-range position was noted in Chapter 4. Most individuals are usually quite weak in the mid-range position of an exercise because it is rarely emphasized. As a repetition variation, the normally brief pause in the mid-range position can be done for a slightly longer duration — perhaps 3-4 seconds. Using an extended pause is also an excellent tool to incorporate when first teaching a youth the idea of pausing in the mid-range position. However, an extended pause in the mid-range position essentially involves a mild isometric muscular contraction that tends to elevate blood pressure. As such, this technique should not be used with youths who suffer from hypertension.

What If It Hurts?

Throughout the course of a program, a youth may not have a full, pain-free range of motion during an exercise — especially in the unfortunate event of a sports injury. There are several different revisions and adjustments that can be made in the basic program design that would enable a youth to continue strength training a certain bodypart in a safe, prudent and pain-free manner. It should be noted that these methods are intended for conditions that aren't viewed as being very serious or extremely painful. Injured youths should be treated by qualified sportsmedicine personnel such as sport physicians, athletic trainers, physical therapists, etc.

Lighten the Resistance
In the event of pain, the first step is to reduce the amount of weight being used. Let's suppose that a youth's patellar tendon hurts when doing leg extensions with the normal training weight. Reducing the amount of weight will produce less stress on the tendon and perhaps allow the youth to perform the exercise in a pain-free manner. The amount that the weight is reduced will depend upon the extent and the nature of the pain.

Reduce the Speed of Movement
If pain-free exercise is still not possible even after reducing the amount of weight, the next maneuver would be to slow down the speed of movement. This may involve raising the weight in about 4-8 seconds instead of the traditional 1-2 seconds. Reducing the speed of movement will decrease the amount of stress placed on a given joint. Slowing down the speed of movement will also necessitate using a reduced amount of weight, thereby lowering the stress even further.

Change the Exercise Angle
If pain persists during certain exercises, the angle at which the movement is normally performed can be changed. This option

can be used with many exercises for the upper body — especially those that involve the shoulder joint. Let's say that a youth has slight shoulder pain when doing a bench press in the supine position (i.e., the torso is positioned level with the ground). In many cases, if the angle of the bench is changed to either an incline or to a decline, there will be less stress on the shoulder joint. Likewise, pain is sometimes felt when performing a seated press with the bar positioned behind the head. The pain is usually alleviated when performing a seated press with the bar positioned in front of the head.

Another exercise that may exacerbate shoulder pain is a behind-the-neck lat pulldown with an overhand grip. Often, the pain is characterized as a tightness or a pinching in the shoulder joint. Generally, the discomfort can be lessened by changing the angle of the pull. This is accomplished by grasping the bar underhanded with the palms facing the torso and pulling the bar to the upper chest instead of behind the neck.

Use a Different Grip

In the case of the shoulder joint, many times there is less stress if a different grip is used. Again, let's say that a youth experiences slight pain when doing an exercise such as a bench press. It is quite possible that there will be a significant reduction in pain by simply changing the grip from that used with a barbell to a parallel grip using dumbbells. It should be noted that any exercise that can be performed with a barbell can also be performed with dumbbells. As such, there is an option for varying the grip used in movements for every major muscle group in the upper torso.

Perform Different Exercises

Another option is to perform different exercises that use the same muscle groups. For instance, if a youth simply cannot perform a lat pulldown without experiencing pain or discomfort, then perhaps a different exercise can be used that works the same muscles in a pain-free manner. In this case, a seated row or a bent over row can be substituted to involve the same muscles as a lat pulldown, namely the upper back, biceps and forearms.

Limit the Range of Motion

There's a possibility that pain occurs only at certain points in the range of motion such as the starting or the mid-range position of the movement. In either case, the range of movement for the exercise can be restricted. For example, if pain occurs at the starting position of a movement, a youth should stop short of a full stretch; similarly, if pain occurs at the mid-range position of an exercise, a youth should stop short of a full muscular contraction. The range of motion can be gradually increased until a full, pain-free range of movement is obtained.

Exercise the Good Limb

If all else fails, the unaffected limb can still be exercised. For example, suppose a youth had knee surgery and, as a result, the left leg was placed in a cast from the mid-thigh to the ankle. Obviously, the youth would not be able to perform any exercises below the left hip joint. However, the youth can still strength train the muscles on the right side of the lower body. Interestingly, research has shown that training a limb on one side of the body will actually increase the strength of the untrained limb on the other side of the body.

Exercise Unaffected Bodyparts

Even though a youth may not be able to exercise an injured area due to an unreasonable amount of pain or discomfort, movements can still be performed for the uninjured bodyparts. If a youth has a knee injury, exercises can still be done for the entire upper torso — assuming, of course, that the exercises are done while sitting or laying down and not while standing. Likewise, a youth with a shoulder injury can still train the muscles of the lower body.

VI. STRENGTH AND CONDITIONING Q & A

There are some final random topics and issues that should be addressed. This chapter examines some of the most frequently asked questions concerning youth strength and conditioning.

1. What precautions should be taken by youths when exercising in hot, humid weather?

The importance of safeguarding the body against heat-related injuries cannot be overemphasized. Younger teens — particularly those who are overweight and those who are unaccustomed to laboring in the heat — are at an increased risk for heat injuries while exercising in hot, humid environments. Potential heat disorders include heat exhaustion, heat stroke and heat cramps.

Youths should gradually acclimatize to heat and humidity. This may necessitate initially performing outdoor activities during the cooler parts of the day (i.e., early morning and late evening). Most adverse reactions to heat and humidity occur during the first few days of exercising outdoors. As youths adapt to hot, humid conditions, they'll be able to exercise at greater levels of intensity while maintaining safe body temperatures. Adequate rest intervals should also be taken.

It's important for youths to rehydrate with cold liquids as needed. Their bodyweight should be measured each day before and after exercising. In this way, water loss can be monitored to determine if adequate rehydration is taking place. About 16 ounces of water should be consumed for every pound of weight that is lost during exercise. Coaches who deny liquids to their athletes under adverse conditions are putting them at risk for a heat disorder.

Lightweight, light-colored clothing that is loose fitting should be worn to promote heat loss. (Lighter colors will reflect the sun's rays; darker colors will absorb them.) Under no circumstances should youths exercise in rubberized clothing or the so-called "sauna suits." Exercising with the body covered in this manner can be lethal since these garments trap perspiration and cause the body to overheat rapidly.

2. What's the correct way to breathe when lifting weights?

It's important for youths to breathe properly while performing a strenuous activity such as strength training — especially during maximal efforts. Holding the breath during exertion creates an elevated pressure in the abdominal and thoracic cavities which is referred to as the Valsalva maneuver. The elevated pressure interferes with the return of blood to the heart. This may deprive the brain of blood and can cause a youth to lose consciousness.

To emphasize correct breathing, exhale when the resistance is raised and inhale when the resistance is lowered. Or, simply remember EOE — Exhale On Effort. As it turns out, inhaling and exhaling naturally usually results in correct breathing.

3. What are the so-called growth plates?

The growth plates are cartilaginous discs that lie between the diaphysis (the central shaft of the bone) and the epiphysis (the end of the long bone). These structures are responsible for longitudinal growth of the immature bone. Longitudinal bone growth ceases when the diaphysis and the epiphysis are united or fused and the disc is replaced by bone. Much of the concern in strength training at an early age focuses on the potential risk of damaging the epiphysis. Excessive loads on immature bones, extreme weight-bearing activities and various overuse injuries associated with highly repetitive activities may interrupt the normal bone growth patterns or predispose a youth to injury.

4. Will plyometrics improve the vertical jump?

Not necessarily. Plyometrics apply to any exercise or jumping drill that uses the myotatic or stretch reflex of a muscle. This particular reflex is triggered when a muscle is pre-stretched prior to a muscular contraction, resulting in a more powerful movement than would otherwise be possible. For example, just before jumping vertically — such as for a rebound — a youth bends at the hips and the knees. This "countermovement" pre-stretches the hip and the leg muscles allowing the youth to generate more force than if the jump were performed without first squatting down. Popular exercises based on this principle include bounding, hopping and various box drills (such as depth jumping). Upper body plyometrics frequently incorporate medicine balls to induce the myotatic reflex.

Clearly, most of the support for plyometrics is based upon personal narratives and sketchy research. There is little scientific evidence that definitively proves plyometrics are productive. While muscular force is certainly increased by the pre-stretch, it doesn't necessarily follow that a training benefit occurs. In fact, one plyometric guru even admits that the information about plyometrics is anecdotal and "methodologically weak."

More importantly, the possibility of injury from plyometrics is positively enormous. A growing number of strength and fitness professionals are questioning the safety of plyometrics. When performing plyometrics, the musculoskeletal system is exposed to repetitive trauma and extreme biomechanical loading. Plyometrics place an inordinate amount of strain on the connective tissues of the lower body. The most common plyometric-related injuries are patellar tendinitis, stress fractures, shin splints and strains of the ankle and the knee. Compression fractures related to the use of plyometrics have also been reported. Other potential injuries include — but aren't limited to — sprains, heel bruises, meniscal (i.e., cartilage) damage and ruptured tendons. Youths are especially vulnerable. It's no surprise that many prominent orthopedic surgeons, physical therapists and athletic trainers view plyometrics as an injury waiting to happen.

Further research is needed to determine if plyometric exercises are safe and effective. At this point, plyometrics have not been proven to be productive and carry an unreasonably high risk of injury. The vertical jump can be improved in a much safer manner by simply practicing jumping skills and techniques in the same way that they are used in the sport and by strengthening the major muscle groups, especially the hips and the legs.

5. When youths stop lifting weights their muscles will turn to fat, right?

Wrong. Muscle cannot be changed into fat — or vice versa — any more than lead can be changed into gold. Muscle tissue consists of special contractile proteins that allow movement to occur. The composition of muscle tissue is about 70 percent water, 22 percent protein and 7 percent fat. Conversely, fatty tissue is composed of spherical cells that are specifically designed to store fat. Fatty tissue is about 22 percent water, 6 percent protein and 72 percent fat. Because muscle and fat are two different and distinct types of biological tissue, muscles can't convert to fat when a youth stops lifting weights. Similarly, lifting weights — or doing any other rigorous activity — won't cause fat to change into muscle. The fact is that muscles atrophy — or become smaller — from prolonged disuse and muscles hypertrophy — or get larger — as a result of physical exercise.

6. Wouldn't it be better for youths to exercise their bodyparts on alternate days instead of doing all of them on one day?

Exercising different bodyparts on alternate days is known as a "split routine." This has been a popular training method of bodybuilders and recreational lifters for many years. In this type of routine, workouts are performed on consecutive days but different muscles are exercised. For example, the muscle groups might be "split" such that the lower body is exercised on Mondays and Thursdays and the upper body is trained on Tuesdays and Fridays.

It's certainly true that a person using a split routine doesn't usually exercise the same muscles two days in a row. However, it takes a minimum of 48 hours in order for the body to replenish its stockpiles of carbohydrates (or glycogen) following an intense workout. (Carbohydrates are the principal fuel during intense exercise.) So, if the lower body was worked out on Monday, the body's carbohydrate stores were depleted. Even if different muscles are trained on Tuesday, the body hasn't had the necessary 48 hours to fully recover those carbohydrate stores.

There may be some individual variations in recovery ability but split routines are generally inappropriate, inefficient and unreasonable for the majority of the population. The quality of work done in the weight room should be emphasized rather than the quantity of work. Remember, the most efficient program is one that produces the maximum possible results in the least amount of time.

7. What exactly are steroids and are they really that harmful?

Steroids are synthetic derivatives of the male sex hormone testosterone. The results of one study indicate that 6.64 percent of twelfth-grade male students either use or have used steroids and that over two thirds of the user group initiated use when they were 16 years of age or younger. Extrapolating these data suggest that 250,000-500,000 adolescents are using or have used steroids.

Michigan State University Strength Coach Ken Mannie says, "The list of adverse effects [from steroid use] reads like a Stephen King horror story." The use of anabolic steroids poses serious threats to the liver (peliosis hepatis and liver tumors — both of which are irreversible and life-threatening as well as jaundice) and the kidneys (kidney stones and Wilm's tumor). In addition, there are risks to the cardiovascular system (increased blood pressure and cholesterol — two major coronary risk factors) and the reproductive system (feminizing side effects in males including a decreased sperm count, testicular atrophy, gynecomastia, a high-pitched voice, sterility, prostate enlargement and functional impotency; masculinizing side effects in females including enlargement of the clitoris, decreased breast size, increased facial and body hair, a deepening of the voice, menstrual irregularities, amenorrhea, an increased risk of breast cancer and uterine atrophy).

The use of steroids — even in low doses — also potentiates certain psychological behavior patterns such as auditory hallucinations of voices, extreme mood swings, sleeping disturbances, euphoria, paranoia, irritability, an increased or a decreased libido, anxiety and delusions. Perhaps the most frequently documented psychological side effect is an increased level of unpredictable hostility and aggression commonly referred to as "roid rage." According to data from the 1991 National Household Survey on Drug Abuse, more than 80 percent of 12- to 17-year-olds who used anabolic steroids stated that they had acted in an aggressive way against people or had committed a crime against property in the previous year. Steroid users may also experience psychological dependency. This can lead to depression-related withdrawal when the use of steroids is discontinued.

Adolescents who use anabolic steroids may experience a premature fusing of their growth plates located in the ends of the long bones. A premature closure of the growth plates before completion of the normal growth cycle will result in stunted growth — which is not reversible.

Steroid users also have a predisposition to tendon and ligament injuries. Users risk blood poisoning and the spread of communicable diseases — including AIDS — from contaminated needles as well as neural dysfunction as a result of improperly placed needles. Additionally, there is a risk of sudden death accompanying injection due to anaphylactic shock.

Other possible side effects are fluid retention, a loss of scalp hair, unprovoked nose bleeds, arthritis, peptic ulcers and acne. Finally, steroid use often leads to multiple drug abuse. Steroid users may start using other drugs in an attempt to control the unwanted side effects of steroid use. For example, amphetamines are taken to combat depression and diuretics are used to avoid fluid retention and to lower the blood pressure.

Under the Anabolic Steroid Control Act of 1990, the use of anabolic steroids is restricted in the same manner as some narcotics, depressants and stimulants. Current legislation has penalties that include a maximum $1,000 fine and a maximum one-year sentence for possession (first offense).

Youths who play around with steroids are gambling with their physical and mental well-being . . . perhaps permanently. It's in a youth's best interests to steer clear of this or any other "performance-enhancing" drug.

To emphasize correct breathing, exhale when the resistance is raised and inhale when the resistance is lowered.

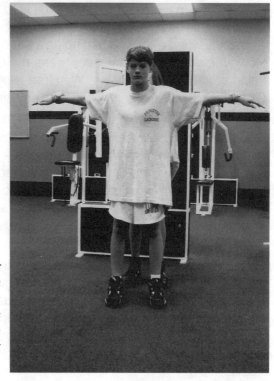

It doesn't matter whether the muscles are fatigued with a resistance that comes from a machine, a barbell, a cinder block or a human being.

8. How often should a youth max out?

Never! Many youths will want to "max out" to see how much weight they can lift for one repetition. There is no need for anyone to perform a one-repetition maximum (1-RM) — particularly a youth. Attempting to see how much weight can be lifted for a 1-RM is dangerous. Performing a 1-RM with heavy weights places an inordinate and unreasonable amount of stress on the muscles, bones and connective tissue. An injury occurs when this stress exceeds the structural integrity of those components. A 1-RM attempt also tends to cause an abnormally high increase in blood pressure. Finally, a 1-RM lift is a highly specialized skill that requires a great deal of technique and practice. The repetition ranges suggested throughout the book will allow youths to exercise their muscles in a safe fashion.

9. Is it better to use free weights (i.e., barbells and dumbbells) or machines?

When using machines, the resistance is balanced which makes the exercise less awkward. This may be advantageous — especially when a youth is beginning a strength training program. However, younger and smaller teens may have a difficult time fitting properly on a machine. With free weights, one size fits all. Other than that, neither modality has any significant advantages over the other.

It should be noted that youths won't develop one way with machines and another way with barbells — assuming that their levels of intensity are similar with both modalities. In addition, improvements in strength can be produced by both types of equipment. Studies have demonstrated no significant differences in strength improvement between groups using free weights and groups using machines.

Recall that a muscle must be fatigued with a workload in order to increase in size and strength. Since muscles don't have a brain, eyeballs or cognitive ability, they can't possibly "know" the source of the workload. So, it doesn't matter whether the muscles are fatigued with a resistance that comes from a machine, a barbell, a cinder block or a human being. The most important controllable factor in determining the response from strength training is the level of intensity — not the equipment that is used. As such, equipment selection should be based upon personal preferences — not personal prejudices.

10. Won't lifting weights make females less flexible and bulk them up?

One of the biggest misconceptions in strength training is the belief that females will lose flexibility and develop large, unsightly muscles. It was noted in Chapter 4 that a properly conducted strength training program does not reduce flexibility. Exercising throughout a full range of motion against a resistance will maintain or even improve flexibility. Females who have residual fears about losing flexibility can perform a comprehensive stretching routine both before and after their strength training program (see Chapter 2). As an added measure, the muscles can also be stretched immediately following the completion of each exercise.

As early as the 1960s, research has demonstrated that females can achieve significant improvements in muscular strength without concomitant gains in muscle size. In one widely referenced study, the largest increase in muscle size experienced by any of the 47 females in the study was less than one-quarter inch. Clearly, strength training does not lead to excessive muscular bulk or produce masculinizing effects in the majority of females.

There are several physiological reasons that prevent or minimize the possibility of a female significantly increasing the size of her muscles. First of all, most females are genetically bound by an unfavorable and unchangeable ratio of muscle to tendon (i.e., short muscle bellies coupled with long tendinous attachments). In addition, compared to males most females have low levels of serum testosterone. The low level of this growth-promoting hormone restricts the degree of muscular hypertrophy in females.

A final physiological factor that prevents or minimizes the possibility of a female significantly increasing her muscular size is her percentage of body fat. Quite simply, females tend to inherit higher percentages of body fat than do males. For example, the average 18- to 22-year-old female is about 22-26 percent body fat, whereas the average male of similar age is about 12-16 percent. This extra body fat tends to soften or mask the effects of strength training. Females who possess very little subcutaneous body fat appear more muscular than they actually are because their muscles are more visible. Similarly, the appearance of muscle mass following a strength training program may not be the result of muscular hypertrophy. Rather, a decrease in subcutaneous fat may simply make the same amount of muscle mass more noticeable.

In the case of female bodybuilders, they inherit a greater potential for muscular hypertrophy than the average female. Highly competitive female bodybuilders have developed large muscles because of their genetic potential. They did not develop large muscles simply because they were engaged in bodybuilding activities.

There is a relatively small number of females who have inherited the potential to experience significant muscular hypertrophy from strength training. However, the majority of females can gain considerable strength from a strength training program yet have little or no change in their muscle mass. In short, it is physiologically improbable for the average female to develop large muscles that are unsightly or "unfeminine."

11. Does the Strength Shoe really work?

The Strength Shoe is a modified athletic shoe with a four-centimeter thick rubber platform attached to the front half of the sole. This attachment prevents the heel from striking the ground during exercises and drills. The shoe is touted as an effective method of increasing ankle flexibility, calf circumference and "speed, quickness and explosive power" when used in a plyometrics-based training protocol. (Question 4 of this chapter discusses plyometrics in greater detail.)

One study found that subjects who performed a 10-minute jump training program in Strength Shoes (or regular athletic shoes for that matter) did not significantly increase their vertical jump height greater than the subjects who acted as controls.

In another study, no enhancement of flexibility, strength or performance was observed for participants wearing the Strength Shoe at the end of the 8-week training program — despite following the suggested protocol of the manufacturers. In this particular study, it's important to note that one third of the subjects who wore the Strength Shoes complained of anterior tibial pain (shin splints) and one subject withdrew from the study because the pain was severe. All of the subjects were previously involved in strenuous activities and none of the subjects reported leg pain prior to the study. Additionally, no subject wearing normal training shoes reported leg pain. As such, the authors felt that "the pain was device-related." In summation, the researchers concluded, "The use of the Strength Shoe cannot be recommended as a safe, effective training method for development of lower leg strength and flexibility."

12. Is the adage "No pain, no gain" really true?

To a degree, yes. The most critical factor in achieving gains in muscular size and strength is the level of intensity or effort. As an exercise becomes more intense, it also becomes more uncomfortable . . . and more painful. The discomfort and pain is related to the high concentration of blood lactic acid (a metabolic byproduct of high intensity, short-duration energy production). However, a youth must differentiate between muscular pain and orthopedic pain. Pain throughout a muscle during intense activity is normal and indicates a high degree of effort. Pain throughout a joint during intense activity is abnormal and indicates a possible orthopedic problem.

13. What strength tests are recommended for checking the progress of youths in the weight room?

Strength testing isn't really necessary to monitor progress. If youths are recording their workout data — and they should — their workout card can simply be checked to evaluate their strength levels. This doesn't mean that strength testing cannot be done — some use it as a motivational tool. That's fine, as long as the strength testing doesn't become a weightlifting meet.

The most popular — and traditional — way to assess muscular strength has been to determine how much weight can be lifted for a one-repetition maximum (1-RM). It's been noted earlier (question 8 of this chapter) that attempting a 1-RM is potentially dangerous. Muscular strength can be measured in a safe and practical — yet reasonably accurate — manner without having someone "max out."

The following mathematical equation can be used to predict a 1-RM based upon repetitions-to-fatigue:

$$\text{Predicted 1-RM} = \frac{\text{Weight Lifted}}{1.0278 - .0278x}$$

where x = the number of repetitions performed

Example: Suppose that a young boy did 10 repetitions-to-fatigue with 100 pounds. First, multiplying .0278 by the number of repetitions [10] equals .278. Subtracting .278 from 1.0278 leaves .7498. Dividing .7498 into the weight lifted [100 pounds] yields a predicted 1-RM of about 133.37 pounds.

In other words, he can do 10 repetitions with about 75 percent (or .7498) of his predicted 1-RM. Regardless of whether his strength increases or decreases, he will always be able to perform exactly 10 repetitions with roughly 75 percent of his maximum. Therefore, if he increases his 10-RM by 20 percent [from 100 to 120 pounds] then he'll also increase his 1-RM by 20 percent [from 133.37 to 160 pounds].

This formula is only valid for predicting a 1-RM when the number of repetitions-to-fatigue is 10 or less. It should also be noted that if the repetitions exceed about 10, then the test becomes less accurate for evaluating muscular endurance as well as for estimating a 1-RM. At any rate, a test of muscular endurance — though not a direct measure of pure maximal strength — is much safer than a 1-RM lift because it involves a submaximal load.

Finally, the purpose of strength testing should not be to compare the strength of one youth to another. It's unfair to make strength comparisons between youths because each person has a different genetic potential for achieving muscular strength.

Strength testing is much more meaningful and fair when a youth's performance is compared to his or her last performance — not to the performance of others.

14. Isn't periodization the most effective way of gaining strength?

Also referred to as "cycling," periodization is a theoretical training schedule of preplanned workouts that have been popularized by weightlifters to peak for a one-repetition maximum (1-RM) during their competition. The idea is to change or "cycle" the number of sets, repetitions and workload of the exercises performed in the weight room. For example, in its simplest form youths might do 3 sets of 10 reps in each exercise with 75 percent of their 1-RM in Week #1, 3 sets of 8 reps with 80 percent of their 1-RM in Week #2 and so on until they are performing a 1-RM.

The concept of periodization is based upon the fact that highly competitive weightlifters peak for only several contests a year. This type of protocol doesn't do much good for a young athlete who might have to peak two or three times a week for several months. Indeed, what competitions does the youth peak for? Aren't they all important? Imagine a youth saying, "Sorry about my performance tonight, Coach, but I'm not scheduled to peak for 10 more days."

In short, trying to implement periodization with individuals other than competitive weightlifters is confusing, impractical and unnecessary. There are more efficient and far less complicated ways of addressing a youth's strength training needs.

15. Are strength training activities recommended for preadolescents?

The term "preadolescents" applies to youths with an upper age limit of about 11 years for girls and 13 years for boys. Strength training activities for preadolescents is controversial. At the present time, there is a lack of substantial information regarding the effectiveness, benefits and risks of strength training by preadolescents. Recent research seems to suggest that preadolescents can attain significant increases in strength provided that the exercises are performed with an adequate level of intensity. However, few studies have explored injury rates. In one of the few studies, 18 preadolescent children showed a significant increase in strength from 30 minutes of strength training activities performed 3 times per week for 14 weeks. The study showed that a short-term, supervised program for preadolescents results in a low injury rate and does not adversely effect bone, muscle or epiphysis nor does it adversely effect growth, flexibility or development.

Nevertheless, additional studies are needed to examine whether or not preadolescents can strength train without risk before such activities gain widespread acceptance. It should also be noted that preadolescents may not possess the level of emotional maturity necessary to understand age-appropriate goals.

In the case of preadolescents, calisthenic-type movements that involve their bodyweight as resistance (such as push-ups and sit-ups) are quite effective for building strength without placing an inordinate amount of stress on their bones and joints.

16. Isn't it true that lifting weights explosively will increase speed and quickness?

No! To decrease the risk of injury, youths should be required to perform each exercise with a controlled speed of movement. Explosive lifting is dangerous. If explosive lifting doesn't cause immediate musculoskeletal damage, it will certainly predispose a youth to future injury.

High-velocity movements are actually less productive than movements performed in a slow, deliberate manner. Here's why: Whenever a weight is lifted explosively, momentum is introduced to provide movement to the weight or resistance. After the initial explosive movement, little or no resistance is encountered by the muscles throughout the remaining range of motion. In simple terms, the weight is practically moving under its own power. To illustrate the effects of momentum on muscular tension, imagine that you pushed a 100 pound cart across the length of a basketball court at a deliberate, steady pace. In this instance, you maintained a constant tension on your muscles for the entire distance. Now,

To decrease the risk of injury, youths should be required to perform each exercise with a controlled speed of movement.

A youth who is unable to perform sit-ups can perform the exercise on a board in a position in which the upper torso is elevated higher than the feet.

suppose that you were to push the cart across the court again. This time, however, you accelerated your pace to the point where you were running as fast as possible. If you were to stop pushing the cart at midcourt, it would continue to move by itself because you gave it momentum. So, in this case, your muscles had resistance over the first half of the court . . . but not over the last half of the court. The same effect occurs in the weight room. When weights are lifted explosively, there is tension on the muscles over the initial part of the movement . . . but not over the last part. In effect, the requirement for muscular force is reduced and so are the potential strength gains.

Explosive lifting can also be dangerous. Dr. Fred Allman, a past president of the American College of Sports Medicine, states, "It is even possible that many injuries . . . may be the result of weakened connective tissue caused by explosive training in the weight room." Using momentum to lift a weight increases the internal forces encountered by a given joint; the faster a weight is lifted, the greater these forces are amplified — especially at the point of explosion. When the forces exceed the structural limits of a joint, an injury occurs in the muscles, bones or connective tissue.

It's much safer and more efficient to raise the weight without any jerking or explosive movements and to lower it under control. Raising the weight in about 1-2 seconds and lowering it in about 3-4 seconds will ensure that the speed of movement is not ballistic in nature and that momentum does not play a significant role in the efficiency of the exercise.

17. Is it okay to perform sit-ups and leg lifts with straight legs?

Sit-ups and leg lifts should never be performed with straight legs. When the legs are straight, the iliopsoas muscle of the frontal hip area is stretched out and it tugs the lumbar spine into an exaggerated curve known as lordosis. This position creates maximal peak compressive and shear forces in the lumbar region. On the other hand, when the knees and the hips are bent and supported, the iliopsoas muscle is relaxed. This flattens the lumbar curvature and decreases the spinal load. Research using computer simulation has shown that compressive forces and shear forces are dramatically reduced during the performance of a sit-up exercise with the hips and the knees flexed at 90 degrees.

Under no circumstances should the so-called "Roman Chair" sit-up be done. This particular movement hyperextends the spine and places undue stress on the low back area which has led to numerous injuries.

18. Are there any exercises in the weight room that should be avoided?

Yes. Youths must avoid movements that place an unreasonable amount of stress on their musculoskeletal system so as not to disturb the growth plates. The American Academy of Pediatrics has noted that the competitive lifting movements have a significant potential for injury in youths. In addition, the American Orthopaedic Society for Sports Medicine — an organization that distinguishes between strength training and weightlifting — contraindicates the competitive lifting movements in training regimens. Numerous scientific, athletic and rehabilitative professionals have also questioned the safety of certain movements done by competitive weightlifters.

Potentially dangerous movements that have been identified as being orthopedically unsafe include plyometrics (see question 4 of this chapter), barbell squats and Olympic-style lifting movements such as power cleans and snatches. Clearly, the potential for injury from most of these exercises is positively enormous.

Most of the exercises used by competitive weightlifters expose the muscles, joints and connective tissue to excessive biomechanical loading that can immediately result in traumatic injuries (e.g., various sprains and strains) or predispose a person to later injuries. The shoulder, elbow, wrist, low back and knee account for most of the injuries

One movement of particular orthopedic concern is the power clean. The power clean is basically the initial phase of a competitive, Olympic-style lift known as the "clean and jerk" and is perhaps the most dangerous exercise a youth can do. A power clean is inherently dangerous because it is performed explosively. (Recall that explosive lifting is also inefficient due to the involvement of momentum.) Power cleans cause repetitive, forced hyperextension of the lumbar spine. This forced hyperextension can lead to any number of injuries and defects, including lumbar sprain, lumbar strain, disc injury and spondylolysis. Excessive impact forces as a result of "catching" the bar could also increase the risk of injury.

Since the early 1960s, the safety of barbell squats has also been questioned by strength and fitness professionals. Squatting with a barbell on the shoulders creates excessive shear forces (i.e., side-to-side) in the knee joint. As the length of the legs increase, so does the shearing or "grinding" effect in the knee — a youth with long legs is more prone to injury than a youth with short legs. In addition, a barbell squat causes compression of the spinal column, which could result in a herniated or ruptured disc. Compression is most evident when the lifter is in the bottom position of the barbell squat, where the anterior aspect of the lumbar vertebrae is compacted and the intervertebral discs are pushed in a posterior direction. Research has revealed that when someone squats with as little as .8 to 1.6 times their bodyweight, the force in the low back region is actually 6 to 10 times their bodyweight. That means that if a youth weighs 140 pounds and does barbell squats with about 112 to 224 pounds, the load on the lumbar area can be anywhere from 840 to 1,400 pounds. The exact amount of force is a function of how far the weight is from the low back, so a youth with a long torso subjects his or her low back to higher forces than a youth with a shorter torso.

Even if a youth has excellent technique, various types of injuries can result from the performance of competitive weightlifting movements. In one study, researchers administered a questionnaire to 71 competitors entered in the 1981 Michigan Teenage Powerlifting Championship. The teenagers sustained 98 injuries relating to powerlifting which caused them to miss 1,126 days of training. The low back region suffered 50 percent of all powerlifting injuries. The incidence of injury related to weight training was also examined in a survey of 354 junior and senior high school football players. This study revealed the most common site of injury was the low back. The power clean, the clean and jerk and the barbell squat accounted for the majority of the injuries.

The same major muscles used in the performance of a power clean and a barbell squat — namely the hips and the legs — can be exercised in a much safer manner with a movement such as a leg press. The message is clear: The competitive lifting movements are potentially dangerous — particularly for youths — and should not be included in a strength training program.

19. What if a youth lacks sufficient muscular strength to perform push-ups and sit-ups?

There are at least two alternatives for a youth who isn't strong enough to perform push-ups. One option is to perform the exercise in the kneeling position. This will increase the youth's leverage and make push-ups easier to perform. As muscular strength improves, the youth can progress to push-ups with straight legs.

A second option is to perform the push-up in a position in which the hands are elevated higher than the feet. As an example, a youth can assume the push-up position with the hands on an inclined sit-up board and the feet on the floor. Again, this will increase the youth's leverage and make the exercise easier to perform. As the youth increases muscular strength, the incline of the board should be decreased until the youth is performing push-ups with the hands and feet on the floor with the body straight. (The hands can be placed on a bench or the seat of a chair if a sit-up board is unavailable.)

This strategy can also be used with a youth who is unable to perform sit-ups. In this instance, the youth would perform sit-ups on the board in a position in which the upper torso is elevated higher than the feet. As abdominal strength improves, the incline of the board should be decreased until the youth is performing sit-ups with the upper torso on the floor.

20. Are protein powders and amino acid supplements recommended as a way of increasing size and strength?

The need for a high intake of dietary protein and/or amino acid supplements has been drastically exaggerated and overrated by health food manufacturers and promoters. The truth is, there is no consistent scientific evidence that indicates a high protein intake or amino acid supplementation improves performance or increases muscle mass. An overwhelming number of researchers, scientists, strength and fitness practitioners, scientific nutritionists, registered dieticians and physicians have noted that a high intake of protein or amino acid supplementation is unnecessary for individuals who consume a well-balanced diet.

Since amino acid supplementation is very expensive, purchasing those products is viewed as a waste of money. In most cases, amino acid supplements are an expensive form of powdered milk. For those who are concerned with getting enough protein in their diet, sufficient protein can be obtained by simply consuming more foods that are high in protein such as meats and fish.

Excessive protein intake does have numerous unwanted side effects — several of which may be physically detrimental and dangerous. A high protein intake in excess of the needs for building body tissue and essential body compounds is either stored as fat or excreted in the urine. Excreting excessive protein in the urine places a heavy burden on the liver and kidneys and may damage those organs.

An excessive intake of protein also increases the risk of dehydration which increases the possibility for developing a heat-related disorder (i.e., heat exhaustion, heat stroke or heat cramps). Other side effects from excessive protein intake include an excessive loss of calcium in the urine, an increased risk of renal disease, diarrhea, cramping, gout and gastrointestinal upset.

The hype-inspired use of amino acid supplements has generated considerable concern for consumer safety. Amino acid supplements taken in large doses are essentially drugs with unknown physical effects. In 1992, the Federation of American Societies for Experimental Biology reviewed the scientific literature on the safety of amino acids and reported that there is insufficient scientific evidence to establish safe levels of intake of the amino acid supplements on the market. Additionally, the American Council of Science and Health recommends, "Unless you are participating in a scientific study conducted by reputable researchers, you should not take amino acid supplements since they have not been proven safe."

Like protein and amino acid supplementation, there is little evidence to suggest that vitamin and mineral supplementation in excess of the Recommended Dietary Allowance (RDA) is needed by those who consume a well-balanced diet. It should also be noted that megadoses of vitamins (i.e., any dose greater than 10 times the RDA) carry a risk of toxicity which can create adverse side effects and may lead to serious medical complications. Though excess amounts of water-soluble vitamins are mainly excreted in the urine, they still may have toxic effects. Of greatest concern is excessive intake of the fat-soluble vitamins, particularly vitamins A and D which can be extremely toxic and may have adverse side effects.

There's no need for supplements provided that a variety of foods that provide adequate calories and nutrients is consumed. Research has concluded that nutritional supplements have little or no positive influence on performance and may even be physiologically damaging. Taking the money used to purchase these expensive supplements and investing it in high-quality foods instead will result in greater success in maximizing potential in a far safer manner.

VII. THE HIPS

Because the lower body has such a large amount of muscle mass, it is generally the most important region in the body. Therefore, a comprehensive strength training workout for youths must address the muscles of the hips.

Hip Muscles

The hip region is made up of 3 major muscle groups: the buttocks, the adductors and the iliopsoas.

Buttocks

The buttocks muscles are the largest and strongest muscles in the body. The buttocks are composed of three main muscle groups: the gluteus maximus, the gluteus medius and the gluteus minimus. The primary function of the gluteus maximus is hip extension (driving the upper leg backward); the main function of the gluteus medius and the gluteus minimus is hip abduction (spreading the legs apart). The "glutes" are important muscles used in running and jumping.

Adductors

The adductor group is composed of five muscles that are located throughout the inner thigh. The adductor magnus is the largest of these muscles. The muscles of the inner thigh are used during adduction of the hip (bringing the legs together).

Iliopsoas

The iliopsoas is a collective term for the two primary muscles of the front hip area: the iliacus and the psoas. The main function of the iliopsoas is to flex the hip (bring the knees to the chest). The iliopsoas plays a major role in many activities such as lifting the knees when walking or running. Because the iliopsoas is often considered with the muscles of the abdomen, exercises for the iliopsoas are discussed with those of the mid-section (Chapter 13).

Hip Exercises

This chapter will describe and illustrate the safest and most productive exercises that youths can perform for their hip muscles using a variety of equipment. Included in the descriptions for each exercise are the muscles used (if more than one muscle is involved, the first muscle listed is the prime mover), the suggested repetitions, the type of movement and performance points for making the exercise safer and more productive. (For help in identifying the muscles, an anatomy chart is shown in the appendix.) The exercises described in this chapter are the leg press, hip abduction and hip adduction.

LEG PRESS

Muscles used: buttocks, hamstrings, quadriceps

Suggested repetitions: 20-25 (younger) or 15-20 (older)

Type of movement: multiple-joint

Performance Points:

- If the machine has an adjustable seat, position it so that the angle between the upper and the lower legs is about 90 degrees in the starting position.
- The feet should be placed on the foot pedal slightly wider than shoulder width apart. If possible, position the lower legs so that they are roughly perpendicular to the base of the foot pedal.
- When performing this movement on a Universal multi-station machine, the upper foot pedals should be used (if provided). The lower foot pedals tend to create excessive shear forces in the knee joint.
- If the machine has hand grips, they should be grasped lightly.
- Extend the feet forward until the legs are almost completely straight in the mid-range position of each repetition.
- Pause briefly in the mid-range position (legs just short of full extension) and then lower the weight under control to the starting position (heels near buttocks) at the completion of every repetition to obtain a proper stretch.

- During the performance of the exercise, force should be exerted through the heels — not through the balls of the feet.
- The knees should not lock or "snap" in the mid-range position of a repetition. This takes the tension off the target muscles and may hyperextend the knees.
- The portion of the weight stack being lifted should not bounce off or slam against the remainder of the weight stack between repetitions.
- This exercise is typically performed with a machine (either selectorized or plate-loading).
- This movement may be done unilaterally (one limb at a time) in the event of a knee injury or a gross strength imbalance. It may also be done in this fashion if a training variation is desired.
- This exercise may be contraindicated for youths with hyperextended knees.

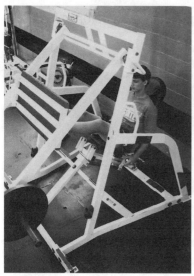

Plate-Loading Machine

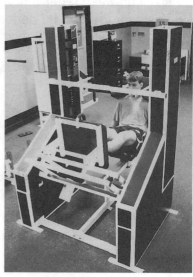

Selectorized Machine

HIP ABDUCTION

Muscles used: hip abductors (gluteus medius)

Suggested repetitions: 15-20 (younger) or 10-15 (older)

Type of movement: single-joint

Performance Points:

- If a machine is used for this movement and it has hand grips, they should be grasped lightly.
- Spread the legs apart as far as possible in the mid-range position of each repetition.
- Pause briefly in the mid-range position (legs apart) and then lower the resistance under control to the starting position (legs together) at the end of every repetition to obtain a proper stretch.
- The body should not bend forward as this exercise is performed.
- The portion of the weight stack being lifted should not bounce off or slam against the remainder of the weight stack between repetitions.
- This exercise can be performed with a selectorized machine or manual resistance.

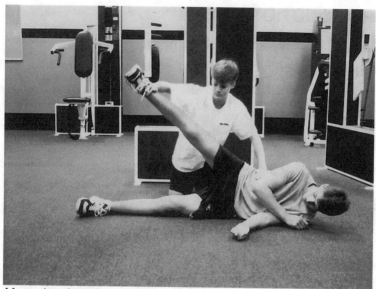

Manual resistance

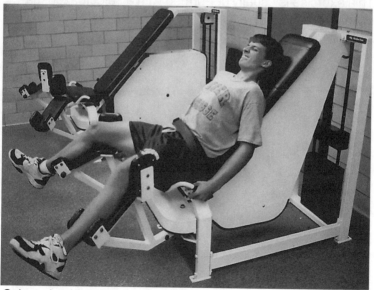

Selectorized machine

HIP ADDUCTION

Muscles used: hip adductors (inner thigh)

Suggested repetitions: 15-20 (younger) or 10-15 (older)

Type of movement: single-joint

Performance Points:

- If a machine is used for this movement and it has hand grips, they should be grasped lightly.
- Bring the legs completely together in the mid-range position of each repetition.
- Pause briefly in the mid-range position (legs together) and then return the resistance under control to the starting position (legs apart) at the completion of each repetition to ensure a proper stretch.
- The portion of the weight stack being lifted should not bounce off or slam against the remainder of the weight stack between repetitions.
- This exercise is usually performed with a selectorized machine or manual resistance.

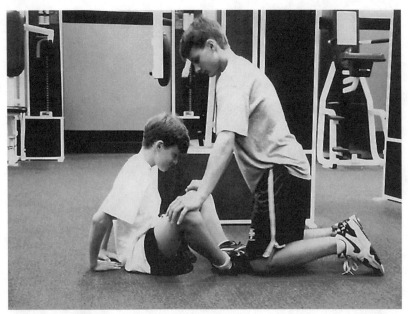

Manual resistance

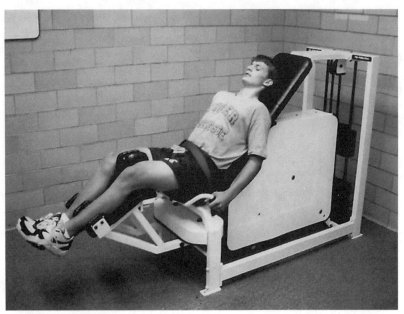

Selectorized machine

VIII. THE LEGS

A considerable amount of muscle mass is located in the upper and the lower legs. Because of this, these muscles should not be neglected in a youth strength training program.

Upper Leg Muscles

The two primary muscle groups of the upper legs are the hamstrings and the quadriceps.

Hamstrings

The "hams" are located on the backside of the upper leg and actually include three separate muscles: the semimembranosus, the semitendinosus and the biceps femoris. Together, these muscles are involved in flexing the lower leg around the knee joint (raising the heel toward the buttocks) and in hip extension. The hamstrings are used during virtually all running and jumping activities. Unfortunately, the muscle is very susceptible to pulls and tears. Strong hamstrings are necessary to balance the effects of the powerful quadriceps muscles.

Quadriceps

The "quads" are the most important muscles on the front part of the thighs. As the name suggests, the quadriceps are made up of four muscles. The vastus lateralis is located on the outside of the thigh; the vastus medialis resides on the inner (medial) side of the thigh above the patella (the kneecap); between these two thigh muscles is the vastus intermedius; and finally, laying on top of the vastus intermedius is the rectus femoris. The main function of the quads is extending (or straightening) the lower leg at the knee joint. The quads are involved in all running, kicking and jumping skills.

Lower Leg Muscles

The calves and the "dorsi flexors" are the 2 major muscle groups in the lower legs.

Calves

Each calf is made up of two important muscles — the gastrocnemius (or "gastroc") and the soleus — which are located on the back side of the lower leg. Sometimes these two muscles are jointly referred to as the "triceps surae" or, more simply, the "gastroc-soleus." The soleus actually resides underneath the gastroc and is used primarily when the knee is bent at 90 degrees or more (e.g., in the seated position). The calves are involved when the foot is extended at the ankle (or when rising up on the toes). The calves play a major role in running and jumping activities.

Dorsi flexors

The front part of the lower leg contains four muscles that are sometimes simply referred to as the "dorsi flexors." The largest of these muscles is the tibialis anterior. The dorsi flexors are primarily used in flexing the foot toward the knee. It is critical to strengthen the dorsi flexors as a safeguard against shin splints.

Leg Exercises

This chapter will describe and illustrate the safest and most productive exercises that youths can perform for their upper and lower leg muscles using a variety of equipment. Included in the descriptions for each exercise are the muscles used (if more than one muscle is involved, the first muscle listed is the prime mover), the suggested repetitions, the type of movement and performance points for making the exercise safer and more productive. (For help in identifying the muscles, an anatomy chart is shown in the appendix.) The exercises described in this chapter are the leg curl, leg extension, calf raise and dorsi flexion.

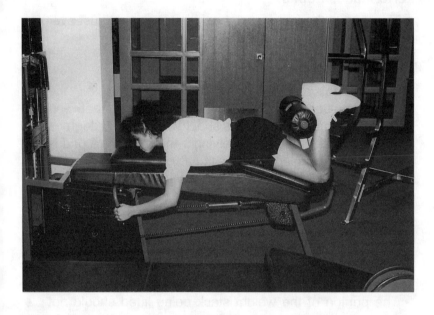

The muscles of the legs should not be neglected in a youth strength training program.

LEG CURL

Muscles used: hamstrings

Suggested repetitions: 15-20 (younger) or 10-15 (older)

Type of movement: single-joint

Performance Points:

- The tops of the kneecaps should be positioned just over the edge of the pad, not on the pad.
- If a machine is used for this movement and it has hand grips, they should be grasped lightly.
- Pull the heels as close to the buttocks as possible in the mid-range position of each repetition. The angle between the upper and the lower legs should be about 90 degrees or less. (This could be deceiving if the machine's pad is "humped" or angled rather than flat.)
- Pause briefly in the mid-range position (heels near buttocks) and then lower the resistance under control to the starting position (legs straight) at the end of each repetition to provide a proper stretch.
- Raising the hips during the performance of this movement is acceptable since this action actually increases the range of motion.
- The portion of the weight stack being lifted should not bounce off or slam against the remainder of the weight stack between repetitions.
- This exercise can be performed sitting, standing or laying prone using a machine (either selectorized or plate-loading) or manual resistance.
- This movement may be done unilaterally (one limb at a time) in the event of a knee injury or a gross strength imbalance. It may also be done in this fashion if a training variation is desired.
- This exercise may be contraindicated for youths with low back pain or hyperextended knees.

Plate-Loading Machine

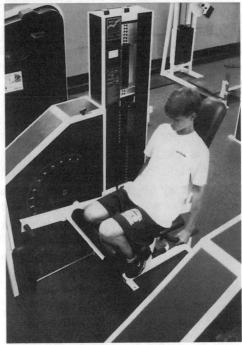

Selectorized Machine

LEG EXTENSION

Muscles used: quadriceps

Suggested repetitions: 15-20 (younger) or 10-15 (older)

Type of movement: single-joint

Performance Points:

- When performing this movement on a machine, there should be little or no space between the backs of the knees and the front edge of the seat pad; likewise, there should be little or no space between the buttocks and the back pad.
- If a machine is used for this movement and it has hand grips, they should be grasped lightly.
- Extend the lower legs up as high as possible in the mid-range position of each repetition.
- Pause briefly in the mid-range position (legs straight) and then lower the weight under control to the starting position (heels near buttocks) at the completion of every repetition to obtain a proper stretch.
- The upper torso should remain against the back pad as this exercise is performed — movement should only occur around the knee joints.
- The portion of the weight stack being lifted should not bounce off or slam against the remainder of the weight stack between repetitions.
- This exercise is usually performed on a machine (either selectorized or plate-loading) or with manual resistance.
- This movement may be done unilaterally (one limb at a time) in the event of a knee injury or a gross strength imbalance. It may also be done in this fashion if a training variation is desired.

Plate-Loading Machine

Selectorized Machine

CALF RAISE

Muscles used: calves

Suggested repetitions: 15-20 (younger) or 10-15 (older)

Type of movement: single-joint

Performance Points:

- Position the balls of the feet on the edge of the step and place the heels over the edge.
- Rise up on the toes as high as possible in the mid-range position of each repetition.
- Pause briefly in the mid-range position (ankles extended) and then lower the weight under control to the starting position (heels near floor) at the end of each repetition to ensure a proper stretch.
- This exercise can be performed sitting or standing using a machine (either selectorized or plate-loading) or by holding a dumbbell in one hand alongside the body.
- The legs should be kept fairly straight while performing the standing calf raise.
- This exercise should not be performed by placing a weight on the shoulders (e.g., either a barbell or a machine's movement arm) since this involves spinal compression.
- This movement may be done unilaterally (one limb at a time) in the event of an ankle injury or a gross strength imbalance. It may also be done in this fashion if a training variation is desired.
- This exercise may be contraindicated for youths with shin splints.

Plate-Loading Machine

Selectorized Machine

DORSI FLEXION

Muscles used: dorsi flexors (tibialis anterior)

Suggested repetitions: 15-20 (younger) or 10-15 (older)

Type of movement: single-joint

Performance Points:

- Pull the foot toward the lower leg as much as possible during each repetition.
- Pause briefly in the mid-range position (ankle flexed) and then return the resistance under control to the starting position (ankle extended) at the end of each repetition to provide a proper stretch.
- After performing a set for one ankle, repeat the exercise for the other ankle.
- This exercise is usually performed on a machine (either selectorized or plate-loading) or with manual resistance.

Manual Resistance

Plate-Loading Machine

IX. THE CHEST

The chest area — along with the upper back and the shoulders — is one of the major muscle groups in the upper torso.

Chest Muscles

The major muscle surrounding the chest area is the pectoralis major. It is thick, flat and fan-shaped and is the most superficial muscle of the chest wall. The pectoralis minor is a thin, flat triangular muscle that is positioned beneath the pectoralis major. The "pecs" pull the upper arm down and across the body. Like most of the upper torso muscles, the pecs are involved in throwing and pushing movements.

Chest Exercise

This chapter will describe and illustrate the safest and most productive exercises that youths can perform for their chest muscles using a variety of equipment. Included in the descriptions for each exercise are the muscles used (if more than one muscle is involved, the first muscle listed is the prime mover), the suggested repetitions, the type of movement and performance points for making the exercise safer and more productive. (For help in identifying the muscles, an anatomy chart is shown in the appendix.) The exercises described in this chapter are the push-up, bench press, incline press, decline press, dip and bent arm fly.

PUSH-UP

Muscles used: chest, anterior deltoid, triceps

Suggested repetitions: 10-15 (younger) or 6-12 (older)

Type of movement: multiple-joint

Performance Points:

- The hands should be positioned on the floor slightly wider than shoulder width apart. An excessively wide hand position should not be used since this will reduce the range of motion.
- Push the body straight up until the arms are almost completely extended in the mid-range position of each repetition.
- Pause briefly in the mid-range position (arms just short of full extension) and then lower the body under control to the starting position (chest touching the floor) at the completion of every repetition to obtain a proper stretch.
- The elbows should not lock or "snap" in the mid-range position of a repetition. This takes the tension off the target muscles and may hyperextend the elbows.
- Avoid arching the lower back during this movement — the upper torso should remain in alignment with the lower body throughout the performance of this movement.
- Placing the hands on elevation pads or wooden blocks permits a better stretch.
- This exercise can be performed using the bodyweight or manual resistance.
- Youths who are unable to do the minimum number of suggested repetitions in strict form using their bodyweight can obtain better leverage by performing this movement in the kneeling position.
- Youths who can perform the maximum number of suggested repetitions or more in strict form using their bodyweight can increase the workload on the muscles by performing the exercise slower or by having a partner apply manual resistance.
- This exercise may be contraindicated for youths with hyperextended elbows.

Bodyweight

Manual Resistance

BENCH PRESS

Muscles used: chest, anterior deltoid, triceps

Suggested repetitions: 10-15 (younger) or 6-12 (older)

Type of movement: multiple-joint

Performance Points:

- The hands should be positioned slightly wider than shoulder width apart. An excessively wide grip should not be used since this will reduce the range of motion.
- Lower the resistance under control to the middle portion of the chest during each repetition.
- Push the hands forward until the arms are almost completely straight in the mid-range position of each repetition.
- The elbows should not lock or "snap" in the mid-range position of a repetition. This takes the tension off the target muscles and may hyperextend the elbows.
- The buttocks should remain against the back pad (or seat pad) throughout the performance of this exercise. In the event of low back pain, the feet may be placed on the end of the back pad or a stool. This will flatten the lumbar area against the back pad and reduce the stress in the lower back region.
- If a barbell is used, the bar should not bounce off the chest.
- The portion of the weight stack being lifted should not bounce off or slam against the remainder of the weight stack between repetitions.
- This exercise can be performed using a barbell, dumbbells or a machine (either selectorized or plate-loading).
- For safety reasons, this exercise should always be performed with a spotter when using a barbell or dumbbells.
- This exercise may be contraindicated for youths with hyperextended elbows.

Barbell

Selectorized Machine

INCLINE PRESS

Muscles used: chest (upper), anterior deltoid, triceps

Suggested repetitions: 10-15 (younger) or 6-12 (older)

Type of movement: multiple-joint

Performance Points:

- The hands should be positioned slightly wider than shoulder width apart. An excessively wide grip should not be used since this will reduce the range of motion.
- Lower the resistance under control to the upper portion of the chest (i.e., near the collarbones) during each repetition.
- Push the hands forward until the arms are almost completely straight in the mid-range position of each repetition.
- The elbows should not lock or "snap" in the mid-range position of a repetition. This takes the tension off the target muscles and may hyperextend the elbows.
- The buttocks should remain against the seat pad throughout the performance of this exercise. In the event of low back pain, the feet may be placed on a stool. This will flatten the lumbar area against the back pad and reduce the stress in the lower back region.
- If a barbell is used, the bar should not bounce off the chest.
- The portion of the weight stack being lifted should not bounce off or slam against the remainder of the weight stack between repetitions.
- This exercise can be performed using a barbell, dumbbells or a machine (either selectorized or plate-loading).
- For safety reasons, this exercise should always be performed with a spotter when using a barbell or dumbbells.
- This exercise may be contraindicated for youths with hyperextended elbows.

Barbell

Selectorized Machine

DECLINE PRESS

Barbell   Dumbbells

Muscles used: chest (lower), anterior deltoid, triceps

Suggested repetitions: 10-15 (younger) or 6-12 (older)

Type of movement: multiple-joint

Performance Points:

- The hands should be positioned slightly wider than shoulder width apart. An excessively wide grip should not be used since this will reduce the range of motion.
- Lower the resistance under control to the lower portion of the chest during each repetition.
- Push the hands forward until the arms are almost completely straight in the mid-range position of each repetition.
- The elbows should not lock or "snap" in the mid-range position of a repetition. This takes the tension off the target muscles and may hyperextend the elbows.
- The buttocks should remain against the back pad (or seat pad) throughout the performance of this exercise.
- If a barbell is used, the bar should not bounce off the chest.
- The portion of the weight stack being lifted should not bounce off or slam against the remainder of the weight stack between repetitions.
- This exercise can be performed using a barbell, dumbbells or a machine (either selectorized or plate-loading).
- For safety reasons, this exercise should always be performed with a spotter when using a barbell or dumbbells.
- This exercise may be contraindicated for youths with hyperextended elbows.

Barbell

Dumbbells

DIP

Muscles used: chest (lower), anterior deltoid, triceps

Suggested repetitions: 10-15 (younger) or 6-12 (older)

Type of movement: multiple-joint

Performance Points:

- Grasp the handles and support the body with the upper and the lower arms bent at about a 90 degree angle. Push the body straight up until the arms are almost completely extended in the mid-range position of each repetition.
- Pause briefly in the mid-range position (arms just short of full extension) and then lower the body under control to the starting position (arms bent about 90 degrees) at the completion of every repetition to obtain a proper stretch.
- The elbows should not lock or "snap" in the mid-range position of a repetition. This takes the tension off the target muscles and may hyperextend the elbows.
- Youths who are unable to do the minimum number of suggested repetitions in strict form using their bodyweight can do this movement on equipment that gives mechanical assistance. (Most selectorized and plate-loading machines allow an individual to choose a resistance that is less than their bodyweight.)
- Youths who are able to do the maximum number of suggested repetitions or more in strict form using their bodyweight can increase the resistance by attaching extra weight to the waist, by performing the exercise slower or by having a partner apply manual resistance.
- After reaching concentric muscular failure, the muscles can be overloaded further by stepping up to the mid-range position and lowering the bodyweight under control to the starting position for 3-5 additional "negative" repetitions.
- This exercise may be contraindicated for youths with hyperextended elbows.

Bodyweight

Selectorized Machine

BENT ARM FLY

Muscles used: chest, anterior deltoid

Suggested repetitions: 10-15 (younger) or 6-12 (older)

Type of movement: single-joint

Performance Points:

- If a machine or manual resistance is used, bring the elbows as close together as possible during each repetition; if dumbbells are used, maintain about a 90 degree angle between the upper and lower arms throughout the exercise. (Imagine hugging a tree.)
- Pause briefly in the mid-range position and then return the resistance under control to the starting position (arms apart) at the end of each repetition to obtain a proper stretch.
- Extending the arms as the dumbbells are raised will turn the bent arm fly into a dumbbell bench press.
- The buttocks should remain against the back pad (or seat pad) throughout the performance of this exercise. In the event of low back pain, the feet may be placed on the end of the back pad or a stool. This will flatten the lumbar area against the back pad and reduce the stress in the lower back region.
- The portion of the weight stack being lifted should not bounce off or slam against the remainder of the weight stack between repetitions.
- This exercise can be performed using dumbbells, a machine (either selectorized or plate-loading) or manual resistance.
- For safety reasons, this exercise should always be performed with a spotter when using dumbbells.
- This movement may be done unilaterally (one limb at a time) on a machine in the event of a shoulder injury or a gross strength imbalance. It may also be done in this fashion if a training variation is desired.
- This exercise may be contraindicated for youths with hyperextended elbows.

Dumbbells

Selectorized Machine

X. THE UPPER BACK

The upper back — along with the chest and the shoulder areas — is one of the major muscle groups in the upper torso.

Upper Back Muscles

The latissimus dorsi is the long, broad muscle that comprises most of the upper back. The "lats" are the largest and widest muscles in the upper body. Their primary function is to pull the upper arm backward and downward. The latissmus dorsi is particularly important in pulling movements and climbing skills. In addition, developing the latissimus dorsi is necessary to provide muscular balance between the upper back and the chest areas.

Upper Back Exercises

This chapter will describe and illustrate the safest and most productive exercises that youths can perform for their upper back muscles using a variety of equipment. Included in the descriptions for each exercise are the muscles used (if more than one muscle is involved, the first muscle listed is the prime mover), the suggested repetitions, the type of movement and performance points for making the exercise safer and more productive. (For help in identifying the muscles, an anatomy chart is shown in the appendix.) The exercises described in this chapter are the lat pulldown, seated row, bent over row, chin and pullover.

LAT PULLDOWN

Muscles used: upper back (lats), biceps, forearms

Suggested repetitions: 10-15 (younger) or 6-12 (older)

Type of movement: multiple-joint

Performance Points:

• The hands should be spaced approximately shoulder width apart with the palms up. Pull the bar (or handles) to the upper part of the chest and rotate the elbows backward in the mid-range position of each repetition.

• Pause briefly in the mid-range position (bar touching the upper chest) and then return the resistance under control to the starting position (arms fully extended) at the end of each repetition to provide a proper stretch.

• Avoid swinging the upper torso back and forth as this exercise is performed — movement should only occur around the shoulder and the elbow joints.

• This exercise can be performed using a machine (either selectorized or plate-loading) or manual resistance.

• Wrist straps can be used if there is difficulty in maintaining a grip on the handles or bar.

• Some handles permit the lifter to use a parallel grip. The hands can also be spaced several inches wider than shoulder width apart with the palms down. In either of these cases, pull the bar (or handles) behind the head and draw the elbows to the sides.

• Regardless of hand positioning, just about any type of pulling movement — whether it be rowing, chinning or any pulldown variation — exercises the upper back, the biceps and the forearms. However, there are differences in the leverage received from these muscles based upon the grip used. Performing a lat pulldown with an underhand grip (palms facing toward the body) is more biomechanically efficient than doing it with either a parallel grip or an overhand grip (palms facing away from the body). With an underhand grip, the forearm bones (the radius and the ulna) run parallel to one another; with an overhand grip, the radius pivots near the elbow and crosses over the ulna forming an "X". When this happens, the bicep tendon wraps around the radius, creating a biomechanical disadvantage and a loss in leverage. This is also true when using these grips during rowing and chinning movements — the same muscles are used but with varying degrees of leverage.

• Overhand lat pulldowns may be contraindicated for youths with shoulder impingement syndrome.

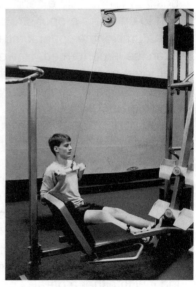

Plate-Loading Machine   *Selectorized Machine*

SEATED ROW

Muscles used: upper back (lats), biceps, forearms

Suggested repetitions: 10-15 (younger) or 6-12 (older)

Type of movement: multiple-joint

Performance Points:

- The grip can be palms up, palms down or parallel depending upon the machine's handles or bar. If manual resistance or Universal equipment is used, pull the movement arm to the mid-section in the mid-range position of each repetition; if a selectorized or a plate-loading machine is used, pull the movement arm to a point just below the shoulders.

- Pause briefly in the mid-range position (hands near torso) and then lower the resistance under control to the starting position (arms fully extended) at the end of each repetition to ensure a proper stretch.

- It's natural for the upper torso to change its position as this exercise is performed. However, avoid swinging the upper torso back and forth as this exercise is performed — movement should only occur around the shoulder and the elbow joints.

- The portion of the weight stack being lifted should not bounce off or slam against the remainder of the weight stack between repetitions.

- This exercise can be performed using a machine (either selectorized or plate-loading) or manual resistance.

- Wrist straps can be used if there is difficulty in maintaining a grip on the handles or bar.

- Performing this movement with an underhand grip (palms facing upward) is more biomechanically efficient than doing it with either a parallel grip (palms facing each other) or an overhand grip (palms facing downward) for the same reason as described in the lat pulldown exercise. However, this movement is still productive when performed with a parallel grip or an overhand grip in the manner described above.

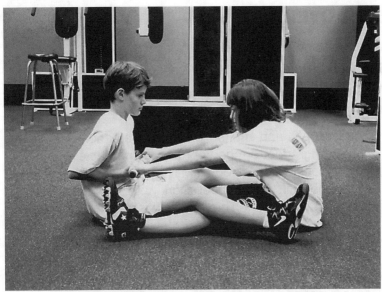

Manual Resistance

Selectorized Machine

BENT OVER ROW

Muscles used: upper back (lats), biceps, forearms
Suggested repetitions: 10-15 (younger) or 6-12 (older)
Type of movement: multiple-joint
Performance Points:

- Place the left hand and the left knee on a bench and position the right foot on the floor at a comfortable distance from the bench. Reach down with the right hand and grasp a dumbbell. Lift the dumbbell slightly off the floor and keep the right arm straight. The right palm should be facing the bench.
- Keeping the upper arm near the torso, pull the dumbbell up to the right shoulder in the mid-range position of each repetition. Pause briefly in the mid-range position (hand near torso) and then return the dumbbell under control to the starting position (arm fully extended) at the end of each repetition to ensure an adequate stretch. After performing a set with the right arm, repeat the exercise with the left arm (with the right hand and the right knee on the bench for support).
- It's natural for the shoulder to change its position as this exercise is performed. However, the movement of the shoulder should not be excessive or used to throw the weight — movement should only occur around the shoulder and the elbow joints.
- This exercise can be performed using a dumbbell or manual resistance.
- Wrist straps can be used if there is difficulty in maintaining a grip on the dumbbell.
- This exercise can also be done with the upper arm and elbow farther away from the torso. This will involve the posterior deltoid and the trapezius to a greater degree. In this case, the upper arm would be almost perpendicular to the torso in the mid-range position and the palm would be facing backward slightly.

Dumbbell

CHIN

Muscles used: upper back (lats), biceps, forearms

Suggested repetitions: 10-15 (younger) or 6-12 (older)

Type of movement: multiple-joint

Performance Points:

- The hands should be spaced approximately shoulder width apart with the palms up. Pull the body upward, touch the upper part of the chest to the bar and rotate the elbows backward in the mid-range position of each repetition. The hands can also be spaced several inches wider than shoulder width apart with the palms down. In this case, the body can be pulled upward so that the bar touches either the upper chest or behind the head and the elbows are drawn to the sides. (This is typically referred to as a "pull-up.")
- Pause briefly in the mid-range position (bar touching the upper chest or behind the head) and then lower the body under control to the starting position (arms fully extended) at the end of each repetition to provide a proper stretch.
- Wrist straps can be used if there is difficulty in maintaining a grip on the bar.
- Performing this movement with an underhand grip (palms facing upward) is more biomechanically efficient than doing it with an overhand grip (palms facing downward) for the same reason as described in the lat pulldown exercise. However, this movement is still productive when performed with an overhand grip in the manner described above.
- Youths who are unable to do the minimum number of suggested repetitions in strict form using their bodyweight can do this movement on equipment that gives mechanical assistance. (Most selectorized and plate-loading machines allow an individual to choose a resistance that is less than their bodyweight.)
- Youths who are able to do the maximum number of suggested repetitions or more in strict form using their bodyweight can increase the resistance by attaching ex-

tra weight to the waist, by performing the exercise slower or by having a partner apply manual resistance.

- After reaching concentric muscular failure, the muscles can be overloaded further by stepping up to the mid-range position and lowering the bodyweight under control to the starting position for 3-5 additional "negative" repetitions.
- Pull-ups (palms down) may be contraindicated for youths with shoulder impingement syndrome.

Bodyweight

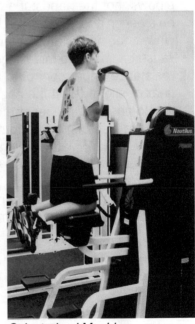

Selectorized Machine

PULLOVER

Dumbbell   Selectorized Machine

Muscles used: upper back (lats)

Suggested repetitions: 10-15 (younger) or 6-12 (older)

Type of movement: single-joint

Performance Points:

- If a machine is used, pull the movement arm to the mid-section in the mid-range position of each repetition. The palms should be kept open and the fingers extended so that force is exerted against the movement arm with the elbows, not the hands; if a dumbbell is used, lay supine on a bench and pull the weight to a position over the chest while keeping the arms relatively straight.
- Pause briefly in the mid-range position and then lower the resistance under control to the starting position (elbows near or slightly past the head) at the end of each repetition to ensure a proper stretch.
- This exercise can be performed using a machine (either selectorized or plate-loading) or a dumbbell.
- The arms should be relatively straight throughout the dumbbell pullover.
- This movement may be contraindicated for youths with low back pain or shoulder impingement syndrome.

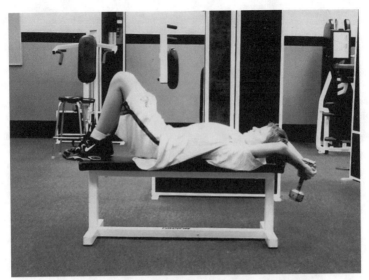

Dumbbell

Selectorized Machine

XI. THE SHOULDERS

The shoulders — along with the chest and the upper back areas — are one of the major muscle groups in the upper torso.

Shoulder Muscles

The primary muscles of the shoulders are the deltoids, the so-called "rotator cuff" and the trapezius.

Deltoids

The "delts" are actually composed of three separate parts or heads. The anterior deltoid is found on the front of the shoulder and is used when raising the upper arm forward; the middle deltoid is found on the side of the shoulder and is involved when the upper arm is lifted sideways (away from the body); the posterior deltoid resides on the back of the shoulder and draws the upper arm backward.

Rotator Cuff

Several other deep muscles of the shoulder are sometimes referred to as the rotator cuff and include the "internal rotators" (the subscapularis and the teres major) and the "external rotators" (the infraspinatus and the teres minor). In addition to performing rotation, these muscles also prevent shoulder impingement. Along with the muscles of the pectoral region, strong shoulders are a vital part of throwing skills and pushing movements.

Trapezius

The trapezius is a kite-shaped (or trapezoid-shaped) muscle that covers the uppermost region of the back and the posterior section of the neck. The primary functions of the "traps" are to elevate the shoulders (as in shrugging), to adduct the scapulae (pinch the shoulder blades together) and to extend the head backward. The trapezius is often considered part of the neck musculature.

Shoulder Exercises

This chapter will describe and illustrate the safest and most productive exercises that youths can perform for their shoulder muscles using a variety of equipment. Included in the descriptions for each exercise are the muscles used (if more than one muscle is involved, the first muscle listed is the prime mover), the suggested repetitions, the type of movement and performance points for making the exercise safer and more productive. (For help in identifying the muscles, an anatomy chart is shown in the appendix.) The exercises described in this chapter are the seated press, lateral raise, front raise, bent over raise, internal rotation, external rotation, upright row and shoulder shrug.

SEATED PRESS

Muscles used: anterior deltoid, triceps

Suggested repetitions: 10-15 (younger) or 6-12 (older)

Type of movement: multiple-joint

Performance Points:

- If a machine with an adjustable seat is used, position it so that the tops of the shoulders are nearly touching the handles; if Universal equipment is used, sit down on the stool facing away from the machine's weight stack.
- Grasp a bar (or handles) and spread the hands slightly wider than shoulder width apart. If a barbell is used, the bar should be placed behind the head on the upper part of the trapezius. Push the bar straight up until the arms are almost completely extended in the mid-range position of each repetition.
- Pause briefly in the mid-range position (arms just short of full extension) and then lower the resistance under control to the starting position (hands near shoulders) at the completion of every repetition to obtain a proper stretch.
- An excessively wide grip should not be used since this will reduce the range of motion.

- The elbows should not lock or "snap" in the mid-range position of a repetition. This takes the tension off the target muscles and may hyperextend the elbows.
- The buttocks should remain flat on the seat pad, the feet kept flat on the floor and the torso kept against the back pad throughout the performance of this exercise. In the event of low back pain, the feet may be placed on a stool (or footrest). This will flatten the lumbar area against the back pad and reduce the stress in the lower back region.
- The portion of the weight stack being lifted should not bounce off or slam against the remainder of the weight stack between repetitions.
- This exercise can be performed using a barbell, dumbbells, a machine (either selectorized or plate-loading) or manual resistance.
- For safety reasons, this exercise should always be performed with a spotter when using a barbell or dumbbells.
- This exercise may be contraindicated for youths with shoulder impingement syndrome. In this case, however, lowering the bar (or handles) in front of the head rather than behind the head will reduce the stress on an impinged shoulder.

Dumbbells   *Selectorized Machine*

LATERAL RAISE

Muscles used: middle deltoid

Suggested repetitions: 10-15 (younger) or 6-12 (older)

Type of movement: single-joint

Performance Points:

- Spread the feet comfortably apart and position the arms along the sides of the body. Keeping the arms fairly straight, raise the resistance away from the sides of the body until the arms are parallel to the floor in the mid-range position of each repetition.
- Pause briefly in the mid-range position (arms parallel to the floor) and then return the resistance to the starting position (arms at the sides) at the end of every repetition to ensure a proper stretch.
- The palms should be facing down in the mid-range position.
- Avoid throwing the resistance by using the legs or by swinging the upper torso back and forth — movement should only occur around the shoulder joints.
- The arms should not be lifted beyond a point that is parallel to the floor.
- This exercise can be performed using dumbbells, a machine (either selectorized or plate-loading) or manual resistance.
- This movement may be done unilaterally (one limb at a time) in the event of a shoulder injury or a gross strength imbalance. It may also be done in this fashion if a training variation is desired.

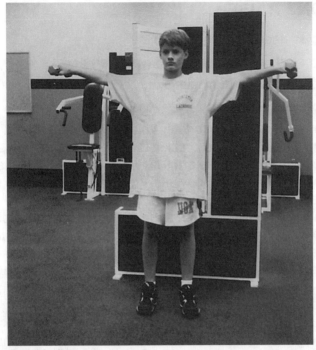

Dumbbells

Manual Resistance

photo by Mark Asanovich

FRONT RAISE

Muscles used: anterior deltoid

Suggested repetitions: 10-15 (younger) or 6-12 (older)

Type of movement: single-joint

Performance Points:

- Spread the feet comfortably apart with one foot slightly in front of the other and position the arms along the sides of the body. Keeping the arms fairly straight, raise the resistance in front of the body until the arms are parallel to the floor in the mid-range position of each repetition.
- Pause briefly in the mid-range position (arms parallel to the floor) and then return the resistance to the starting position (arms at the sides) at the end of every repetition to ensure a proper stretch.
- The palms should be facing each other in the mid-range position.
- Avoid throwing the resistance by using the legs or by swinging the upper torso back and forth — movement should only occur around the shoulder joints.
- The arms should not be lifted beyond a point that is parallel to the floor.
- This exercise can be performed using dumbbells or manual resistance.
- This movement may be done unilaterally (one limb at a time) in the event of a shoulder injury or a gross strength imbalance. It may also be done in this fashion if a training variation is desired.

Dumbbells

Manual Resistance

BENT OVER RAISE

Muscles used: posterior deltoid, trapezius

Suggested repetitions: 10-15 (younger) or 6-12 (older)

Type of movement: single-joint

Performance Points:

- Lay prone on a bench with the shoulders slightly over the edge. Keeping the arms fairly straight and perpendicular to the torso, raise the resistance upward until the arms are parallel to the floor in the mid-range position of each repetition.
- Pause briefly in the mid-range position (arms parallel to the floor) and then lower the resistance under control to the starting position (arms hanging down) at the end of each repetition to ensure a proper stretch.
- The palms should be facing down in the mid-range position.
- Avoid throwing the resistance by swinging the upper torso back and forth — movement should only occur around the shoulder joints.
- This exercise can be performed using dumbbells or manual resistance.
- This movement may be done unilaterally (one limb at a time) in the event of a shoulder injury or a gross strength imbalance. It may also be done in this fashion if a training variation is desired.

Dumbbells

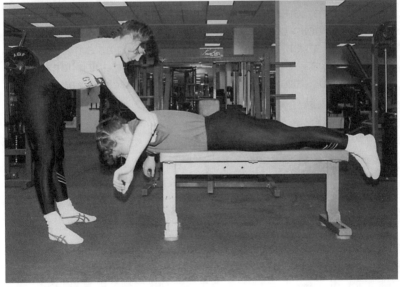

Manual Resistance

INTERNAL ROTATION

Muscles used: internal rotators

Suggested repetitions: 12-15 (younger) or 8-12 (older)

Type of movement: single-joint

Performance points:

- Bend the right arm so that the angle between the upper and the lower arms is about 90 degrees. Without moving the right elbow or changing the angle of the right arm, pull the resistance toward the body in the mid-range position of each repetition.

- Pause briefly in the mid-range position (hand near torso) and then return the resistance under control to the starting position (hand away from torso) at the completion of each repetition to ensure a sufficient stretch.

- After performing a set for the right shoulder, repeat the exercise for the left shoulder.

- This exercise can be performed using a dumbbell, a machine (either selectorized or plate-loading) or manual resistance.

- This movement can also be performed with surgical tubing or elastic cord as the resistance. The tubing is secured to an object that will not move such as a machine. Simply grasp the free end of the tubing and pull it horizontally across the body in the fashion described above. In this case, the movement can be done while standing.

Dumbbell

Manual Resistance

EXTERNAL ROTATION

Muscles used: external rotators

Suggested repetitions: 12-15 (younger) or 8-12 (older)

Type of movement: single-joint

Performance points:

- Bend the right arm so that the angle between the upper and the lower arms is about 90 degrees. Without moving the right elbow or changing the angle of the right arm, push the resistance away from the body in the mid-range position of each repetition.

- Pause briefly in the mid-range position (hand away from torso) and then return the resistance under control to the starting position (hand near torso) at the end of every repetition to obtain a proper stretch.

- After performing a set for the right shoulder, repeat the exercise for the left shoulder.

- This exercise can be performed using a dumbbell, a machine (either selectorized or plate-loading) or manual resistance.

- This movement can also be performed with surgical tubing or elastic cord as the resistance. The tubing is secured to an object that will not move such as a machine. Simply grasp the free end of the tubing and pull it horizontally across the body in the fashion described above. In this case, the movement can be done while standing.

Dumbbell

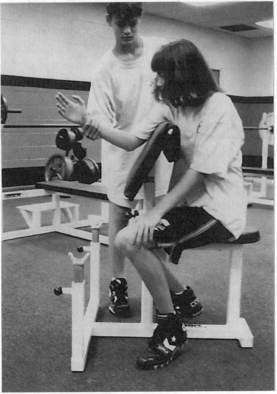

Manual Resistance

UPRIGHT ROW

Muscles used: trapezius, biceps, forearms

Performance Points:

- Spread the feet comfortably apart. Space the hands about 8-10 inches apart with the palms facing the thighs. Pull the resistance up until the hands are approximately level with the shoulders in the mid-range position of each repetition. The elbows should be slightly higher than the hands in this position.

- Pause briefly in the mid-range position (hands near shoulders) and then return the resistance under control to the starting position (arms fully extended) at the end of each repetition to provide a proper stretch.

- Avoid throwing the weight by using the legs or by swinging the upper torso back and forth — movement should only occur around the shoulder and the elbow joints.

- For better biomechanical leverage, the resistance should be kept close to the body as this movement is performed.

- Wrist straps can be used if there is difficulty in maintaining a grip.

- This exercise can be performed using a barbell, dumbbells or a machine (either selectorized or plate-loading).

- This exercise may be contraindicated for youths with shoulder impingement syndrome. In this case, however, pulling the bar to the lower portion of the chest rather than to the upper portion of the chest will reduce the stress on an impinged shoulder. This exercise may also be contraindicated for youths with low back pain.

Barbell

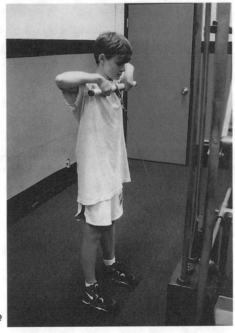

Selectorized Machine

SHOULDER SHRUG

Muscles used: trapezius

Suggested repetitions: 12-15 (younger) or 8-12 (older)

Type of movement: single-joint

Performance Points:

- Spread the feet comfortably apart. Use an alternating grip or a grip with both palms facing backward when using a barbell or Universal equipment; use a parallel grip with other equipment.
- Keeping the arms and the legs straight, pull the resistance up as high as possible trying to touch the shoulders to the ears (as if to say, "I don't know") in the mid-range position of each repetition.
- Pause briefly in the mid-range position (shoulders near ears) and then lower the weight under control to the starting position at the completion of each repetition to obtain an adequate stretch.
- It's not necessary or advisable to "roll" the shoulders during the performance of this exercise.
- Avoid throwing the weight by using the legs or by swinging the upper torso back and forth — movement should only occur around the shoulder joints.
- For better biomechanical leverage, the resistance should be kept close to the body as this movement is performed.
- Wrist straps can be used if there is difficulty in maintaining a grip.
- This exercise can be performed using a barbell, dumbbells or a machine (either selectorized or plate-loading).
- This exercise may be contraindicated for youths with low back pain.

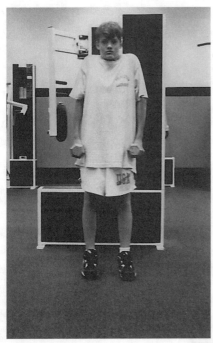

Dumbbells

Selectorized Machine

XII. THE ARMS

The upper and the lower arms contain a relatively small amount of muscle mass and are regarded as the "weak links" in multiple-joint movements for the upper torso. Therefore, it's critical for youths to exercise these smaller, weaker muscles in order to strengthen the weak link.

Upper Arm Muscles

The two primary muscle groups of the upper arms are the biceps and the triceps.

Biceps
The biceps brachii is the prominent muscle on the front part of the upper arm. It causes the arm to flex (or bend) at the elbow. As the name suggests, the biceps has two separate heads. The separation can sometimes be seen as a groove on a well-developed arm when the biceps are fully flexed. The biceps assist the upper torso muscles — especially the lats — in pulling movements and climbing skills.

Triceps
The triceps brachii is a horseshoe-shaped muscle located on the back of the upper arm. This muscle has three distinct heads -- the long, the lateral and the medial. The primary function of the triceps is to extend (or straighten) the arm at the elbow. The triceps assist the upper torso muscles in throwing skills and pushing movements.

Lower Arm Muscles

The forearms are the major muscles in the lower arms.

Forearms
Each forearm is made up of 19 different muscles. These muscles may be divided into two groups on the basis of their position and

functions. The anterior group on the front part of the forearm causes flexion and pronation (turning the palm downward); the posterior group on the back part of the forearm causes extension and supination (turning the palm upward). The forearms effect the wrists and hands, which are important in pulling movements, climbing skills and tasks that involve gripping.

Arm Exercises

This chapter will describe and illustrate the safest and most productive exercises that youths can perform for their arm muscles using a variety of equipment. Included in the descriptions for each exercise are the muscles used (if more than one muscle is involved, the first muscle listed is the prime mover), the suggested repetitions, the type of movement and performance points for making the exercise safer and more productive. (For help in identifying the muscles, an anatomy chart is shown in the appendix.) The exercises described in this chapter are the bicep curl, tricep extension, wrist flexion and wrist extension.

BICEP CURL

Muscles used: biceps, forearms

Suggested repetitions: 10-15 (younger) or 6-12 (older)

Type of movement: single-joint

Performance Points:

• The hands should be spaced about shoulder width apart with the palms up. Pull the bar (or handles) below the chin by bending the arms in the mid-range position of each repetition.

• Pause briefly in the mid-range position (hands near shoulders) and then lower the resistance under control to the starting position (arms straight) at the completion of each repetition to provide a proper stretch.

• Avoid throwing the weight by using the legs or by swinging the upper torso back and forth — movement should only occur around the elbow joints.

• The portion of the weight stack being lifted should not

bounce off or slam against the remainder of the weight stack between repetitions.

- This movement may be done unilaterally (one limb at a time) in the event of an elbow injury or a gross strength imbalance. It may also be done in this fashion if a training variation is desired.
- This exercise can be performed sitting or standing using a barbell, dumbbells, a machine (either selectorized or plate-loading) or manual resistance.
- This exercise may be contraindicated for youths with hyperextended elbows.

Barbell

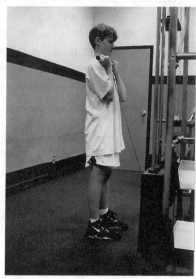

Selectorized Machine

TRICEP EXTENSION

Muscles used: triceps

Suggested repetitions: 10-15 (younger) or 6-12 (older)

Type of movement: single-joint

Performance Points:

- The hands should be spaced about 4-6 inches apart. Extend the arms in the mid-range position of each repetition.
- Pause briefly in the mid-range position (arms fully extended) and then return the weight under control to the starting position (arms bent) at the completion of each repetition to obtain a proper stretch.
- Avoid using the shoulders to lift the weight — movement should only occur around the elbow joints.
- The portion of the weight stack being lifted should not bounce off or slam against the remainder of the weight stack between repetitions.
- This movement may be done unilaterally (one limb at a time) in the event of an elbow injury or a gross strength imbalance. It may also be done in this fashion if a training variation is desired.
- This exercise can be performed sitting, standing or laying supine using a barbell, dumbbells, a machine (either selectorized or plate-loading) or manual resistance.
- This exercise may be contraindicated for youths with shoulder impingement syndrome.

Selectorized Machine

Barbell

WRIST FLEXION

Muscles used: wrist flexors

Suggested repetitions: 12-15 (younger) or 8-12 (older)

Type of movement: single-joint

Performance Points:

- The hands should be spaced about 4-6 inches apart with the palms facing upward and the thumbs alongside the fingers. The forearms can be positioned directly over the upper legs or flat on the bench (between the legs). In this position, the forearms should be roughly parallel to the floor. (This may require placing a pad underneath the feet.) Lean forward slightly so that the angle between the upper and the lower arms is about 90 degrees or less. The wrists should be over the kneecaps (or over the edge of the bench if the forearms are placed on the bench).

- Pull the bar up as high as possible during in the mid-range position of each repetition.

- Pause briefly in the mid-range position and then lower the resistance under control to the starting position (wrists extended) at the end of each repetition to provide a sufficient stretch.

- Placing the thumbs underneath the bar alongside the fingers will permit a greater range of motion.

- The forearms should remain directly over the upper legs throughout the performance of this exercise. The elbows should not flare out to the sides.

- Avoid throwing the weight by using the legs or by swinging the upper torso back and forth -- movement should only occur around the wrist joints.

- This exercise can be performed using a barbell, dumbbells, a machine (either selectorized or plate-loading) or manual resistance.

- This movement may be done unilaterally (one limb at a time) in the event of a wrist injury or a gross strength imbalance. It may also be done in this fashion if a training variation is desired.

Barbell

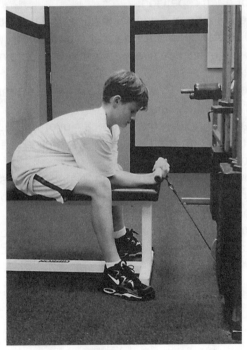

Selectorized Machine

WRIST EXTENSION

Muscles used: wrist extensors

Suggested repetitions: 12-15 (younger) or 8-12 (older)

Type of movement: single-joint

Performance Points:

- Grasp the dumbbell with the right palm facing downward. The forearm can be positioned directly over the right upper leg or flat on the bench (between the legs). In this position, the right forearm should be roughly parallel to the floor. (This may require placing a pad underneath the feet.) Lean forward slightly so that the angle between the upper and the lower arm is about 90 degrees or less. The right wrist should be over the right kneecap (or over the edge of the bench if the forearm is placed on the bench).

- Pull the dumbbell up as high as possible in the mid-range position of each repetition.

- Pause briefly in the mid-range position and then lower the dumbbell under control to the starting position (wrist extended) at the end of every repetition to obtain an adequate stretch.

- After performing a set for the right forearm, repeat the exercise for the left forearm.

- The forearm should remain directly over the upper leg throughout the performance of this exercise. The elbow should not flare out to the side.

- Avoid throwing the weight by using the legs or by swinging the upper torso back and forth — movement should only occur around the wrist joint.

- This exercise is more comfortable when it is performed one limb at a time with a dumbbell rather than both limbs at a time with a barbell.

Dumbbell

XIII. THE MID-SECTION

The muscles of the mid-section — the abdominals and the lower back — serve as a link between the lower body and the upper torso.

Abdominal Muscles

The abdominal muscles are located on the anterior portion of the mid-section and are comprised of the rectus abdominis, the obliques and the transverse abdominis. These muscles perform a variety of functions.

Rectus Abdominis

This long, narrow muscle extends vertically across the front of the abdomen from the lower rim of the rib cage to the pelvis. Its main function is to pull the torso toward the lower body. The fibers of this muscle are interrupted along their course by three horizontal fibrous bands, which give rise to the phrase "washboard abs" when describing an especially well-developed abdomen. The rectus abdominis helps to control the breathing and plays a major role in forced expiration during intense exercise.

Obliques

The external and internal obliques lie on both sides of the waist. The external oblique is a broad muscle whose fibers form a V across the front of the abdominal area, extending diagonally downward from the lower ribs to the pubic bone. The main function of this muscle is to bend the upper torso to the same side and to rotate the torso to the opposite side. The internal obliques lie immediately under the external obliques on both sides of the abdomen. The fibers of the internal obliques form an inverted V along the front of the abdominal wall, extending diagonally upward from the pubic bone to the ribs. The internal obliques bend the upper body to the same side and turn the torso to the same side. The obliques are used in movements in which the upper torso twists or rotates.

Transverse Abdominis

The innermost layer of the abdominal musculature is the transverse abdominis. Its fibers run horizontally across the abdomen. The primary function of the transverse abdominis is to constrict the abdomen. This muscle is also involved in forced expiration and in control of breathing.

Iliopsoas

The iliopsoas is sometimes considered with the muscles of the hips. Its function and anatomical position were discussed previously in Chapter 7.

Lower Back Muscles

The lower back muscles are located on the posterior portion of the mid-section. Low back pain is one of the most common and costly medical problems today. It has been estimated that 8 out of 10 people will experience low back pain sometime in their lives with annual costs of more than 50 billion dollars. Insufficient strength seems to be a factor related to low back pain.

Erector Spinae

The "spinal erectors" make up the main muscle group in the lower back. Their primary purpose is to extend (or straighten) the upper torso from a bent-over position.

Mid-Section Exercises

This chapter will describe and illustrate the safest and most productive exercises that youths can perform for their mid-section muscles using a variety of equipment. Included in the descriptions for each exercise are the muscles used (if more than one muscle is involved, the first muscle listed is the prime mover), the suggested repetitions, the type of movement and performance points for making the exercise safer and more productive. (For help in identifying the muscles, an anatomy chart is shown in the appendix.) The exercises described in this chapter are the sit-up, side bend, knee-up and back extension.

The muscles of the mid-section serve as a link between the lower body and the upper torso.

SIT-UP

Muscles used: rectus abdominis

Suggested repetitions: 12-15 (younger) or 8-12 (older)

Type of movement: single-joint

Performance Points:

- If this exercise is performed on a Universal station, lay supine on the sit-up board and place the feet underneath the roller pads. The angle between the upper and lower legs should be about 90 degrees. Fold the arms across the chest and lift the head off the board. If a selectorized machine is used, sit down and place the upper torso against the back pad. Place the feet underneath the roller pads (if available) and grasp the handles.
- Pull the torso forward until it is almost to the upper legs in the mid-range position of each repetition.
- Pause briefly in the mid-range position (torso near upper legs) and then lower the weight under control to the starting position at the end of every repetition to provide a proper stretch.
- Avoid throwing the arms or snapping the head forward as this exercise is performed — movement should only occur around the mid-section.
- The knees should always be bent when performing this movement to reduce the stress on the lower back.
- To maintain tension on the muscles throughout the sit-up movement, the shoulders should not touch the floor between repetitions.
- This exercise can be performed using the bodyweight, a machine (either selectorized or plate-loading) or manual resistance.
- A partial sit-up — typically referred to as a "crunch" or a "trunk curl" — can be more effective than a full sit-up. To perform a trunk curl, lay on the floor and place the backs of the lower legs on a bench or a stool. The angle between the upper and the lower legs should be about 90 degrees. Likewise, the angle between the upper legs and

the upper torso should be about 90 degrees. Fold the arms across the chest, lift the head off the floor and perform the movement as described above.

- Under no circumstances should the so-called "Roman Chair" sit-up be done. This particular movement hyperextends the spine and places undue stress on the low back area which has led to numerous injuries.
- This exercise may be contraindicated for youths with low back pain.

Bodyweight

Selectorized Machine

SIDE BEND

Muscles used: obliques

Suggested repetitions: 12-15 (younger) or 8-12 (older)

Type of movement: single-joint

Performance Points:

- Spread the feet about shoulder width apart. Hold a dumb-bell or a wrist strap handle in the right hand with the palm facing the outside of the right leg. Place the left palm against the left side of the head. Without moving the hips, bend the upper torso to the right as far as possible.
- Without moving the hips, pull the upper torso to the left as far as possible in the mid-range position of each repetition.
- Pause briefly in the mid-range position and then lower the resistance under control to the starting position at the end of every repetition to ensure a sufficient stretch.
- After performing a set for the left side of the mid-section, repeat the exercise for the right side of the mid-section.
- It's natural for the hips to change their position as this exercise is performed. However, the movement of the hips should not be excessive or used to throw the resistance — movement should only occur around the mid-section.
- Avoid bending forward at the waist while performing this exercise.
- The feet should remain flat on the floor throughout the performance of this movement.
- This exercise can be performed using a dumbbell or a selectorized machine.
- This exercise may be contraindicated for youths with low back pain.

Dumbbell

Selectorized Machine

KNEE-UP

Muscles used: rectus abdominis (lower), iliopsoas

Suggested repetitions: 12-15 (younger) or 8-12 (older)

Type of movement: single-joint

Performance Points:

- Hold onto the bars or handle(s) and cross the ankles.
- Bring the knees as close to the chest as possible in the mid-range position of each repetition.
- Pause briefly in the mid-range position (upper legs near torso) and then lower the legs under control to the starting position (legs straight) at the end of each repetition to obtain a proper stretch.
- Avoid throwing the legs up by swinging the hips back and forth — movement should only occur around the mid-section.
- Youths who are unable to do the minimum number of suggested repetitions in strict form using their bodyweight can do this movement on a sit-up board. As their strength improves, the angle of the board can be increased thereby making the exercise more difficult. Once the greatest height is no longer a challenge, youths can progress to knee-ups from a hanging position.
- Youths who are able to do the maximum number of suggested repetitions or more in strict form using their bodyweight can increase the resistance by performing the exercise slower or by having a partner apply manual resistance.
- This exercise can be performed using the bodyweight or manual resistance.
- If this movement is done on a sit-up board, the knees should remain bent throughout the entire range of motion.
- Under no circumstances should leg lifts be done with straight legs while laying prone on the floor. This particular movement hyperextends the spine and places undue stress on the low back area which has led to numerous injuries.

Bodyweight

Bodyweight

BACK EXTENSION

Muscles used: erector spinae (low back)

Suggested repetitions: 15-20 (younger) or 10-15 (older)

Type of movement: single-joint

Performance Points:

- If this exercise is performed on a selectorized machine, position the legs underneath the front roller pads (if provided) and the upper back against the rear roller pad. Interlock the fingers and place the palms against the midsection; if this exercise is done on a Universal station or similar freestanding equipment, position the pelvis on top of the hip pad. Allow the upper torso to hang straight down over the edge of the hip pad and fold the arms across the chest.

- Extend the upper torso backward in the mid-range position of each repetition. On the Universal station (or similar equipment), the torso should not be lifted beyond a point that is parallel to the floor.

- Pause briefly in the mid-range position (upper torso away from upper legs) and then lower the resistance under control to the starting position at the end of each repetition to provide a proper stretch.

- Avoid throwing the upper torso or snapping the head backward as this exercise is performed — movement should only occur around the mid-section.

- This exercise may be contraindicated for youths with low back pain.

Bodyweight

Selectorized Machine

XIV. THE NECK

It is extremely important to strengthen the neck muscles of youths who participate in combative sports such as football, wrestling, boxing and judo. A strong neck will protect the cervical area from traumatic injury.

Neck Muscles

The primary muscles of the neck are the strenocleidomastoideus, the trapezius and the neck extensors.

Sternocleidomastoideus

This muscle has two parts or heads located on each side of the neck, which start behind the ears and run down to the sternum (breastbone) and clavicles (collarbones). When both sides contract at the same time, the sternocleidomastoideus flexes the head toward the chest; when one side acts singly, it brings the head laterally toward the shoulder or rotates the head to the side.

Trapezius

The anatomical position and muscular functions of the trapezius were described previously in Chapter 11.

Neck Extensors

A number of muscles reside on the posterior section of the neck. These muscles can simply be referred to as the "neck extensors." Their primary function is to extend the head backward.

Neck Exercises

This chapter will describe and illustrate the safest and most productive exercises that youths can perform for their neck muscles using a variety of equipment. Included in the descriptions for each exercise are the muscles used (if more than one muscle is involved, the first muscle listed is the prime mover), the suggested repetitions, the type of movement and performance points for making the exercise safer and more productive. (For help in identifying the muscles, an anatomy chart is shown in the appendix.) The exercises described in this chapter are the neck extension, neck flexion and neck lateral flexion.

NECK EXTENSION

Muscles used: trapezius, neck extensors

Suggested repetitions: 12-15 (younger) or 8-12 (older)

Type of movement: single-joint

Performance Points:

• When using a machine, adjust the seat so that the back of the head is centered on the head pads when sitting upright. Place the feet flat on the floor, grasp the handles lightly and bend the head forward. When using manual resistance, lay prone on a bench and position the body so that the head hangs over the edge. Place the hands and the feet on the floor (or position the legs across the edge of the bench).

• Extend the head backward as far as possible in the mid-range position of each repetition.

• Pause briefly in the mid-range position (head away from chest) and then lower the head under control to the starting position (chin near chest) at the end of each repetition to obtain a proper stretch.

• If the buttocks come off the seat, it means that the legs are being used to help lift the weight.

• The portion of the weight stack being lifted should not bounce off or slam against the remainder of the weight stack between repetitions.

• This exercise can be performed using a machine (either selectorized or plate-loading) or manual resistance.

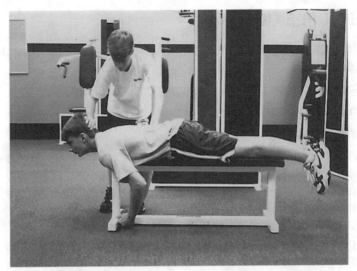

Manual Resistance

Plate-Loading Machine

NECK FLEXION

Muscles used: sternocleidomastoideus (both sides acting together)

Suggested reps: 12-15 (younger) or 8-12 (older)

Type of movement: single-joint

Performance Points:

• When using a machine, adjust the seat so that the face is centered on the head pads when sitting upright. Place the feet flat on the floor, grasp the handles lightly and move the head backward until it is perpendicular to the floor. When using manual resistance, lay supine on a bench, place the feet flat on the floor and position the body so that the head hangs over the edge. Interlock the fingers and place them across the chest.

• Bring the head as close to the chest as possible in the mid-range position of each repetition.

• Pause briefly in the mid-range position (chin near chest) and then lower the head back to the starting position (head perpendicular to the floor) at the end of each repetition to obtain a proper stretch.

• If the buttocks come off the seat, it means that the legs are being used ot help lift the weight.

• The portion of the weight stack being lifted should not bounce off or slam against the remainder of the weight stack between repetitions.

• This exercise can be performed using a machine (either selectorized or plate-loading) or manual resistance.

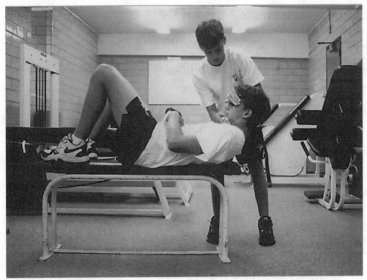

Manual Resistance

Plate-Loading Machine

NECK LATERAL FLEXION

Muscles used: sternocleidomastoideus (one side acting singly)
Suggested reps: 12-15 (younger) or 8-12 (older)
Type of movement: single-joint
Performance Points:

- When using a machine, adjust the seat so that the right side of the face is centered on the head pads when sitting upright. Place the feet flat on the floor, grasp the handles lightly and position the left side of the head near the left shoulder. When using manual resistance, lay on your left side on a bench.
- Without significantly moving the upper torso, bring the head as close to the right shoulder as possible in the mid-range position of each repetition.
- Pause briefly in the mid-range position (head near the right shoulder) and then return the head back to the starting position (head near the left shoulder) at the completion of each repetition to provide a proper stretch.
- After performing a set for right side of the neck, repeat the exercise for the left side of the neck.
- The upper torso should not move significantly as this exercise is performed — movement should only occur around the neck.
- If the buttocks come off the seat, it means that the legs are being used to help lift the weight.
- The portion of the weight stack being lifted should not bounce off or slam against the remainder of the weight stack between repetitions.
- This exercise can be performed using a machine (either selectorized or plate-loading) or manual resistance.

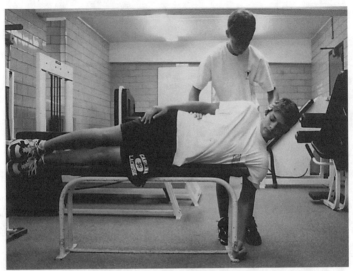

Manual Resistance

Plate-Loading Machine

REFERENCES

Allman, F. L. 1976. Prevention of sports injuries. *Athletic Journal* 56 (March): 74.

American Academy of Pediatrics. 1983. Weight training and weight lifting: Information for the pediatrician. *The Physician and Sportsmedicine* 11 (3): 157-161.

——. 1990. Strength training, weight and power lifting and bodybuilding by children and adolescents. *Pediatrics* 86 (5): 801-803.

American College of Sports Medicine [ACSM]. 1987. Position stand on the use of anabolic-androgenic steroids in sports. *Medicine and Science in Sports and Exercise* 19: 534-539.

——. 1990. Position statement on the recommended quantity and quality of exercise for developing and maintaining cardiorespiratory and muscular fitness in healthy adults. *Medicine and Science in Sports and Exercise* 22: 265-274.

——. 1991. *Guidelines for graded exercise testing and exercise prescription.* 4th ed. Philadelphia: Lea & Febiger.

Ben-Ezra, V. 1992. Assessing physical fitness. In *The Stairmaster fitness handbook*, ed. J. A. Peterson and C. X. Bryant, 91-108. Indianapolis: Masters Press.

Bloch, G. B. 1990. Programs get youths to shape up. *The New York Times* 140 (November 27): C9, col. 1.

Brady, T. A., B. R. Cahill and L. M. Bodnar. 1982. Weight training-related injuries in the high school athlete. *The American Journal of Sports Medicine* 10: 1-5.

Brown, E. W., and R. G. Kimball. 1983. Medical history associated with adolescent powerlifting. *Pediatrics* 72 (5): 636-644.

Brown, T., R. Yost and R. F. McCarron. 1990. Lumbar ring apophyseal fracture in an adolescent weightlifter. *American Journal of Sports Medicine* 18 (5): 533-535.

Brzycki, M. M. 1995. *A practical approach to strength training.* 3d ed. Indianapolis: Masters Press.

———. 1994. Youth fitness: Looking backward and ahead. *Pennsylvania Journal of Health, Physical Education, Recreation & Dance* 64 (3): 24-26.

Brzycki, M. M., and S. Brown. 1993. *Conditioning for basketball.* Indianapolis: Masters Press.

Buckley, W. E., C. E. Yesalis, K. E. Friedl, W. A. Anderson, A. L. Streit and J. E. Wright. 1988. Estimated prevalence of anabolic steroid use among male high school students. *Journal of the American Medical Association* 260 (23): 3441-3445.

Cappozzo, A., F. Felici, F. Figura and F. Gazzani. 1985. Lumbar spine loading during half-squat exercises. *Medicine and Science in Sports and Exercise* 17: 613-620.

Cook, S. D., G. Schultz, M. L. Omey, M. W. Wolfe and M. F. Brunet. 1993. Development of lower leg strength and flexibility with the strength shoe. *The American Journal of Sports Medicine* 21: 445-448.

Cooper, K. H. 1982. *The aerobic program for total well-being.* New York, NY: M. Evans & Co.

Crouch, J. E. 1978. *Functional human anatomy.* 3d ed. Philadelphia: Lea & Febiger.

Diange, J. 1984. Football & power cleans: A dangerous mixture. *Scholastic Coach* 53 (January): 22, 74.

Duda, M. 1988. Plyometrics: A legitimate form of power training? *The Physician and Sportsmedicine* 16 (3): 213-216, 218.

Fox, E. L., and D. K. Mathews. 1981. *The physiological basis of physical education and athletics.* 3d ed. Philadelphia: Saunders College Publishing.

Frankel, V. H., and M. Nordin. 1980. *Basic biomechanics of the skeletal system.* Philadelphia: Lea & Febiger.

Freeman, W. H. 1977. *Physical education in a changing society.* Boston: Houghton Mifflin Company.

Garrett Jr, W. E., and T. R. Malone, eds. 1988. *Muscle development: Nutritional alternatives to anabolic steroids.* Columbus, OH: Ross Laboratories.

Goldman, R. M., P. Bush and R. Klatz. 1984. *Death in the locker room.* South Bend, IN: Icarus Press.

Goldman, R. M., and R. Klatz. 1992. *Death in the locker room: Drugs & sports.* Chicago: Elite Sports Medicine Publications, Inc.

Granhed, H., and B. Morelli. 1988. Low back pain among retired wrestlers and heavyweight lifters. *The American Journal of Sports Medicine* 16: 530-533.

Graves, J. E., and M. L. Pollock. 1992. Understanding the physiological basis of muscular fitness. In *The Stairmaster fitness handbook,* ed. J. A. Peterson and C. X. Bryant, 39-52. Indianapolis: Masters Press.

Horrigan, J., and D. Shaw. 1990. Plyometrics: The dangers of depth jumps. *High Intensity Training Newsletter* 2 (4): 15-21.

Howley, E. T., and B. D. Franks. 1992. *Health fitness instructor's handbook.* 2d ed. Champaign, IL: Human Kinetics Publishers, Inc.

Hutchins, K. 1992. *Super Slow: The ultimate exercise protocol.* 2d ed. Casselberry, FL: Super Slow Systems.

Ivy, J. L. 1991. Muscle glycogen synthesis before and after exercise. *Sports Medicine* 11 (1): 6-19.

Jaworski, R. 1989. Young America sagging. *The New York Times* 138 (March 19): Sec. 4, E27, col. 2.

Jesse, J. P. 1977. Olympic lifting movements endanger adolescents. *The Physician and Sports Medicine* 5 (9): 61-67.

——. 1979. Misuse of strength development programs in athletic training. *The Physician and Sports Medicine* 7 (10): 46-50, 52.

Johnson, C., and J. G. Reid. 1991. Lumbar compressive and shear forces during various trunk curl-up exercises. *Clinical Biomechanics* 6: 97-104.

Kennedy, J. F. 1960. The soft American. *Sports Illustrated* 13 (December 26): 15-17.

Klein, K. K. 1962. Squats right. *Scholastic Coach* 32 (2): 36-38, 70-71.

Kotani, P. T., N. Ichikawa, W. Wakabayashi, T. Yoshii and M. Koshimune. 1971. Studies of spondylolysis found among weightlifters. *British Journal of Sports Medicine* 6: 4-8.

Kulund, D. N., J. B. Dewey, C. E. Brubaker and J. R. Roberts. 1978. Olympic weight-lifting injuries. *The Physician and Sports Medicine* 6 (11): 111-116, 119.

Lambrinides, T. 1990. Playing the percentages: Is it a good or bad idea? *High Intensity Training Newsletter* 2 (4): 12-13.

Leistner, K. E. 1987. Coaches' corner: Periodization for football. *The Steel Tip* 3 (August): 1-3.

——. 1989. Explosive training: Not necessary. *High Intensity Training Newsletter* 1 (2): 3-5.

LeSuer, D. A., and J. H. McCormick. 1993. Prediction of a 1-RM bench press and 1-RM squat from repetitions to fatigue using the Brzycki formula. Abstract presented at the National Strength and Conditioning Association 16th National Conference. Las Vegas, NV.

Lillegard, W. A., and J. D. Terrio. 1994. Appropriate strength training. *Sports Medicine* 78: 457-477.

Lindh, M. 1980. Biomechanics of the lumbar spine. In *Basic biomechanics of the skeletal system*, by V. H. Frankel and M. Nordin, 255-290. Philadelphia: Lea & Febiger.

Mannie, K. 1989. What coaches and athletes should know about steroids! *Scholastic Coach* 59 (September): 50-52.

———. 1990. Strength training follies: The All-P.U.B. Team. *High Intensity Training Newsletter* 2 (2): 11-12.

———. 1991. Roid roulette: A dangerous game. Toledo, OH: Media Production Group. Videotape.

———. 1993. Lift risks are a weighty matter. *NCAA News* 30 (January 27): 4-5.

———. 1994. Some thoughts on explosive weight training. *High Intensity Training Newsletter* 5 (1 & 2): 13-18.

Manuel, D. 1991. Getting kids in shape. *The Boston Globe* 240 (December 1): 65-67.

Mazur, L. J., R. J. Yetman and W. L. Risser. 1993. Weight training injuries: Common injuries and preventative measures. *Sports Medicine* 16: 57-63.

McArdle, W. D., F. I. Katch and V. L. Katch. 1986. *Exercise physiology: Energy, nutrition and human performance.* 2d ed. Philadelphia: Lea & Febiger.

Mussen, P. H., J. J. Conger and J. Kagan. 1979. *Child development and personality.* 5th ed. New York, NY: Harper & Row, Publishers, Inc.

Norris, C. M. 1993. Abdominal muscle training in sport. *British Journal of Sports Medicine* 27: 19-27.

Peterson, J.A., and C. X. Bryant, eds. 1992. *The Stairmaster fitness handbook.* Indianapolis: Masters Press.

Pezullo, D., S. Whitney and J. Irrgang. 1993. A comparison of vertical jump enhancement using plyometrics and strength footwear shoes versus plyometrics alone. *Journal of Orthopaedic and Sports Physical Therapy* 17: 68.

Piehl, K. 1974. Glycogen storage and depletion in human skeletal muscle fibers. *Acta Physiologica Scandinavica* (Supplementum 402): 1-32.

Raithel, K. S. 1988. Are American children really unfit? (Part 1 of 2). *The Physician and Sportsmedicine* 16 (October): 146-154.

Rasch, P. J., and F. L. Allman. 1972. Controversial exercises. *American Corrective Therapy Journal* 26 (4): 95-98.

Rians, C. B., A. Weltman, B. R. Cahill, C. A. Janney, S. R. Tippett and F. I. Katch. 1987. Strength training for prepubescent males: Is it safe? *The American Journal of Sports Medicine* 15: 483-489.

Rice, E. A., J. L. Hutchinson and M. Lee. 1987. *A brief history of physical education.* 5th ed. New York: John Wiley & Sons.

Rice, S. G. 1993. Strength training in young athletes. In *Sports medicine secrets*, ed. M. B. Mellion, 68-71. Philadelphia: Hanley & Belfus, Inc.

Riley, D. 1982. *Maximum muscular fitness: How to develop strength without equipment.* West Point, NY: Leisure Press.

———. 1982. *Strength training by the experts.* 2d ed. West Point, NY: Leisure Press.

Risser, W. L. 1991. Weight training injuries in children and adolescents. *American Family Physician* 44 (6): 2104-2110.

Risser, W. L., J. M. H. Risser and D. Preston. 1990. Weight training injuries in adolescents. *The American Journal of Diseases of Children* 144: 1015-1017.

Ross, J. G., and R. R. Pate. 1987. The national children and youth fitness study II: A summary of findings. *Journal of Physical Education, Recreation and Dance* 58 (November/December): 51-56.

Rossi, F. 1978. Spondylolysis, spondylolisthesis and sports. *Journal of Sports Medicine and Physical Fitness* 18: 317-340.

Rossi, F., and S. Dragoni. 1990. Lumbar spondylolysis: Occurrence in competitive athletes. *Journal of Sports Medicine and Physical Fitness* 30: 450-452.

Skinner, J. S. 1992. Cardiorespiratory fitness. In *The Stairmaster fitness handbook*, ed. J. A. Peterson and C. X. Bryant, 29-37. Indianapolis: Masters Press.

Small, C. L. 1992. Low back problems in young athletes. *High Intensity Training Newsletter* 3 (4): 7-9.

Smith, N. J. 1984. Children and parents: Growth, development, and sports. In *Sports medicine*, ed. R. H. Strauss, 207-217.   Philadelphia: W. B. Saunders Company.

Tanner, S. M. 1993. Weighing the risks: Strength training for children and adolescents.   *The Physician and Sportsmedicine* 21 (6): 105-106, 109-110, 114-116.

Vorobyev, A. N. 1988. Weightlifting injuries and their prevention. *Tyazhelaya Atletika* 1: 239-242.

Welday, J. 1986. Coming clean on the power clean. *Scholastic Coach* 56 (September): 22-23.

Wells, J. B., E. Jokl and J. Bohanen. 1963. The effect of intensive physical training upon body composition of adolescent girls. *Journal of the Association for Physical and Mental Rehabilitation* 17: 68-72.

Westcott, W. L. 1983. *Strength fitness: Physiological principles and training techniques.* Expanded ed. Boston: Allyn and Bacon, Inc.

———. 1986. Integration of strength, endurance and skill training. *Scholastic Coach* 55 (May/June): 74.

Wikgren, S. 1988. The plyometrics debate. *Coaching Women's Basketball* 1 (May/June): 10-13.

Wilmore, J. H. 1982. *Training for sport and activity: The physiological basis of the conditioning process.* 2d ed. Boston: Allyn and Bacon, Inc.

Wolf, M. D. 1982. Muscles: Structure, function and control. In *Strength training by the experts*, 2d ed, by D. P. Riley, 27-40. West Point, NY: Leisure Press.

Yesalis, C. E., N. J. Kennedy, A. N. Kopstein and M. S. Bahrke.   1993. Anabolic-androgenic steroid use in the United States. *Journal of the American Medical Association* 270 (10): 1217-1221.

Appendix

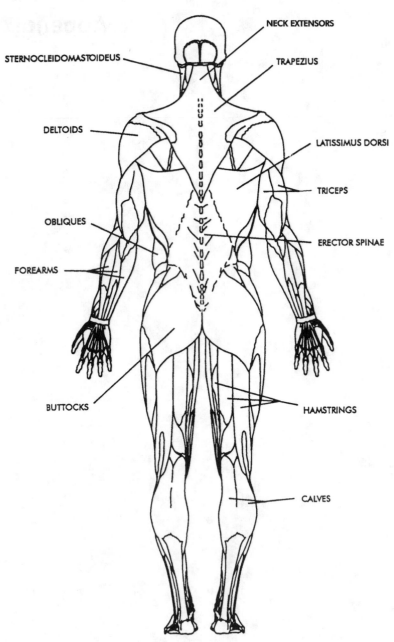

NECK EXTENSORS

STERNOCLEIDOMASTOIDEUS

TRAPEZIUS

DELTOIDS

LATISSIMUS DORSI

TRICEPS

OBLIQUES

ERECTOR SPINAE

FOREARMS

BUTTOCKS

HAMSTRINGS

CALVES

Posterior view of the muscles of the body

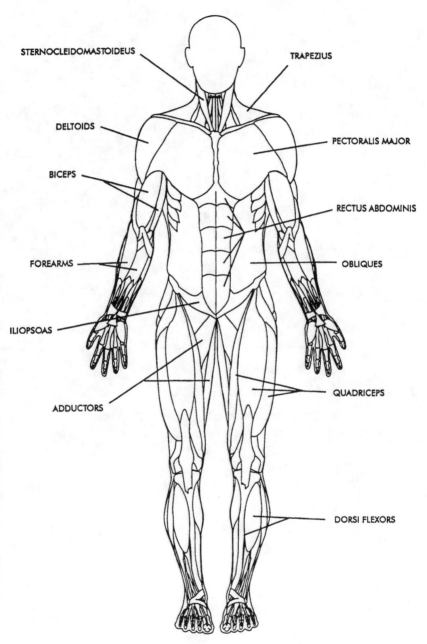

STERNOCLEIDOMASTOIDEUS

TRAPEZIUS

DELTOIDS

PECTORALIS MAJOR

BICEPS

RECTUS ABDOMINIS

FOREARMS

OBLIQUES

ILIOPSOAS

QUADRICEPS

ADDUCTORS

DORSI FLEXORS

Anterior view of the muscles of the body

BIOGRAPHY

Matt Brzycki received his Bachelor of Science degree in Health and Physical Education from the Pennsylvania State University in 1983. He represented the university for two years in the Pennsylvania State Collegiate Powerlifting Championships. Brzycki served as a health fitness supervisor at Princeton University (NJ) from 1983-84. From 1984-90, he was the Assistant Strength Coach at Rutgers University (NJ). In 1990, he returned to Princeton University as the school's Strength Coach and Health Fitness Coordinator. He was named the Coordinator of Health Fitness, Strength and Conditioning Programs at Princeton University in 1994. Brzycki developed the Strength Training Theory and Applications course for exercise science and sports studies majors at Rutgers University and has taught the program since 1990. He will begin teaching the same course at Trenton State College in 1996.

Brzycki has authored over 145 articles that have been featured in more than two dozen different publications. He has also authored the book *A Practical Approach to Strength Training*

Photo by Audrey Grimaldi

(third edition) and coauthored the book *Conditioning for Basketball* with Shaun Brown. (Both books published by Masters Press.)

Prior to attending college, Brzycki served in the U.S. Marine Corps from 1975-79 which included a tour of duty as a drill instructor. He and his wife, Alicia, currently reside in Hamilton Township, New Jersey.